Kleinfeld, J. (1975). Effective teachers of Eskimo and Indian students. *The School Review, 83*(2), 301–344.

Kozol, J. (2006). *The shame of the nation: The restoration of apartheid schooling in America.* Three Rivers Press.

Ladson-Billings, G. (1995). Toward a theory of culturally relevant pedagogy. *American Educational Research Journal, 32*(3), 465–491.

Ladson-Billings, G. (2006). From the achievement gap to the education debt: Understanding achievement in U.S. schools. *Educational Researcher, 35*(7), 3–12.

Ladson-Billings, G. (2009). *The dreamkeepers: Successful teachers of African American children.* Jossey-Bass.

Ladson-Billings, G. & Dixson, A. (2022). Put some respect on the theory: Confronting distortions of culturally relevant pedagogy. In C. Compton-Lilly, T. L. Ellison, K. Perry & P. Smagorinsky (Eds.), *Whitewashed critical perspectives: Restoring the edge to edgy ideas* (pp. 122–137). Routledge.

Lankshear, C. & McLaren, P. L. (1993). *Critical literacy: Politics, praxis, and the postmodern.* SUNY Press.

Lazar, A. (2004). *Learning to be literacy teachers in urban classrooms: Stories of growth and change.* International Reading Association.

Lazar, A. (2022). Apprenticing for equity literacy teaching: A needed change in teacher education. *Journal of Literacy Research, 54*(2), 158–181.

Leonard, A. M. & Woodland, R. H. (2022). Anti-racism is not an initiative: How professional learning communities may advance equity and social–emotional learning in schools. *Theory into Practice, 61*(2), 212–223.

Leung, C. T. (2021). *What I see: Anti-Asian racism from the eyes of a child.* LegaC Publishing.

Lewis, C. (1993). "Give people a chance": Acknowledging social differences in reading. *Language Arts, 70*(6), 454–461.

Lewis, R. D. (2018). *When cultures collide: Leading across cultures.* Nicholas Brealey.

Lewison, M., Flint, A. S. & Van Sluys, K. (2002). Taking on critical literacy: The journey of newcomers and novices. *Language Arts, 79*(5), 382–392.

Love, B. L. (2019). *We want to do more than survive: Abolitionist teaching and the pursuit of educational freedom.* Beacon Press.

Macedo, S. (2000). *Diversity and distrust: Civic education in a multicultural democracy.* Harvard University Press.

Mandela, N. (1990, June 23). *Speech to Madison Park High School, Boston, MA.* Retrieved from https://www.youtube.com/watch?v=b66c6OkMZGw.

Matsuda, M. J. (1991). Voices of America: Accents, antidiscrimination law, and a jurisprudence for the last reconstruction. *The Yale Law Journal, 100*(5), 1329–1407.

Mau, R. Y. (1992). The validity and devolution of a concept: Student alienation. *Adolescence, 27*(107), 731–741.

McDaniel, C. (2006). *Critical literacy: A way of thinking, a way of life.* Peter Lang.

McIntosh, K., Moss, E., Nunn, R. & Shambaugh, J. (2020, February 27). *Examining the Black-white wealth gap.* Brookings. https://www.brookings.edu/blog/up-front/2020/02/27/examining-the-black-white-wealth-gap/

McLaren, P. (1994). *Life in schools: An introduction to critical pedagogy in the foundations of education* (2nd ed.). Longman.

McLean, C. A., Boling, E. C. & Rowsell, J. (2009). Engaging diverse students in multiple literacies in and out of school. In L. Morrow, R. Rueda & D. Lapp (Eds.), *Handbook of research on literacy instruction: Issues of diversity, policy, and equity*. Guilford.

Meacham, J. (2022). *And there was light: Abraham Lincoln and the American struggle*. Random House.

Milner, H. R., IV. (2015). *Rac(e)ing to class: Confronting poverty and race in schools and classrooms*. Harvard Education Press.

Milner, H. R., IV. (2017). Race, talk, opportunity gaps, and curriculum shifts in teacher education. *Literacy Research: Theory, Method, and Practice, 66*, 73–94.

Milner, H. R., IV. (2019). Race to improve teacher education: Building awareness for instruction practice. *American Educator, 43*(3), 13–17.

Milner, H. R., IV. (2020). Disrupting racism and whiteness in researching a science of reading. *Reading Research Quarterly, 55*(S1), S249–S253.

Mobe, T. (n.d.). *Eight African proverbs that every global citizen should know*. Global Citizen. https://www.globalcitizen.org/en/content/africa-proverbs-global-citizens-action-end-poverty/

Moll, L., Amanti, C. N. D. & González, N. (1992). Funds of knowledge for teaching: Using a qualitative to connect homes and schools. *Theory into Practice, 31*(2), 132–141.

Morrow, L. Rueda, R. & Lapp, D. (2009). *Handbook of research on literacy instruction: Issues of diversity, policy, and equity*. Guilford.

Muhammad, G. E. (2020). *Cultivating genius: An equity framework for culturally and historically responsive literacy*. Scholastic, Inc.

Muhammad, G. E. & Haddix, M. (2016). Centering Black girls' literacies: A review of literature on the multiple ways of knowing of Black girls. *English Education, 48*(4), 299–336.

National Council of Teachers of English [NCTE]. (2018). The Black girls' literacies collective statement. *Research in the Teaching of English, 53*(2), 173–175.

National Council of Teachers of English [NCTE]. (2020). *Literacy is more than just reading and writing*. Retrieved from https://ncte.org/blog/2020/03/literacy-just-reading-writing/

Nieto, S. (2000). *Affirming diversity: The sociopolitical context of multicultural education* (3rd ed.). Addison Wesley Longman, Inc.

Nieto, S. (2005). *Affirming diversity*. Pearson Education.

Oakes, J. & Lipton, M. (2002). *Teaching to change the world*. McGraw-Hill.

O'Dell, S. (1992). *Thunder rolling in the mountains*. Dell Yearling Paperback.

Paris, D. (2012). Culturally sustaining pedagogy: A needed change in stance, terminology, and practice. *Educational Researcher, 41*(3), 93–97.

Paris, D. & Alim, H. S. (2014). What are we seeking to sustain through culturally sustaining pedagogy? A loving critique forward. *Harvard Educational Review, 84*(1), 85–100.

Parks, R. & Reed, G. J. (1996). *Dear Mrs. Parks: A dialogue with today's youth*. Lee & Low Books.

Parsons, E. F. (2019). *Ku-Klux: The birth of the Klan during Reconstruction*. The University of North Carolina Press.

Patterson Williams, A. D., Higgs, J. M, Athanases, S. Z., Caraballo, L. & Martinez, D. C. (2020). Noticing for equity to sustain multilingual literacies. *Journal of Adolescent & Adult Literacy, 63*(4), 457–461.

Patton, L. D., Farmer-Hinton, R. L., Lewis, J. D. & Rivers, I. (2010). *"Dear Mr. Kozol": Four African American women scholars and the reauthoring of Savage Inequalities.* Paper presented at the annual meeting of the American Educational Research Association, Denver, CO.

Picower, B. (2021). *Reading, writing, and racism: Disrupting whiteness in teacher education and the classroom.* Beacon Press.

Pierson, R. (2013, May). *Every kid needs a champion.* [Video]. TED Conferences. https://www.ted.com/talks/rita_pierson_every_kid_needs_a_champion?language=en

Plough, B. & Garcia, R. (2015). Whole school English learner reform: A heuristic approach to professional learning in middle schools. *Planning and Changing, 46*(1), 21–41.

Poston, W. S. C. (1990). The biracial identity development model: A needed addition. *Journal of Counseling and Development, 69*(2), 152–155.

Price-Dennis, D. & Muhammad, G. E. (2021). *Black girl's literacies: Transforming lives and literacy practices.* Routledge.

Price-Dennis, D. & Sealy-Ruiz, Y. (2021). *Advancing racial literacies in teacher education: Activism for equity in digital spaces.* Teachers College Press.

Purcell-Gates, V. (1996). Stories, coupons, and the *TV Guide*: Relationships between home literacy experiences and emergent literacy knowledge. *Reading Research Quarterly, 31*(4), 406–428.

Reece, R. L. (2019). Color crit: Critical *Race Theory* and the history and future of colorism in the United States. *Journal of Black Studies, 50*(1), 3–25.

Roberts, M. A. (2010). Toward a theory of culturally relevant critical teacher care: African American teachers' definitions and perceptions of care for African American students. *Journal of Moral Education, 39*(4), 449–467.

Rodriguez, J. P. (2006). Encyclopedia of Slave Resistance and Rebellion [2 volumes]: Greenwood Milestones in African American History. Greenwood.

Rogers, R. & Mosley, M. (2006). Racial literacy in a second-grade classroom: Critical Race Theory, whiteness studies and literacy research. *Reading Research Quarterly, 41*(4), 462–495.

Rolon-Dow, R. (2005). Critical care: A color(full) analysis of care narratives in the schooling experiences of Puerto Rican girls. *American Educational Research Journal, 42*(1), 77–111.

Rosa, J. & Flores, N. (2017). Unsettling race and language: Toward a raciolinguistic perspective. *Language in Society, 46*(5), 621–647.

Rosales, J. & Walker, T. (2021). The racist beginnings of standardized testing. National Education Association. Retrieved from https://www.nea.org/advocating-for-change/new-from-nea/racist-beginnings-standardized-testing

Sachs, J. (2022). *Steep rise in gag orders, many sloppily drafted.* Pen America. https://pen.org/steep-rise-gag-orders-many-sloppily-drafted/

Saint-Louis, T. (2023, January 4). *Best female rappers of 2022.* HipHopDX. https://hiphopdx.com/editorials/best-female-rappers-of-2022

Schussler, D. L. (2006). Defining dispositions: Wading through murky waters. *The Teacher Educator, 41*(4), 251–268.

Sealy-Ruiz, Y. (2021). The critical literacy of race: Toward racial literacy in urban teacher education. In *Handbook of urban education* (pp. 281–295). Routledge.

Seaton, E. K. (2009). Perceived racial discrimination and racial identity profiles among African American adolescents. *Cultural Diversity and Ethnic Minority Psychology, 15*(2), 137.

Shollenberger, T. L. (2015). Racial disparities in school suspension and subsequent outcomes: Evidence from the National Longitudinal Study of Youth. In D. J. Losen (Ed.), *Closing the school discipline gap: Equitable remedies for excessive exclusion* (pp. 31–43). New York: Teachers College Press.

Siddle Walker, V. (1996). *The highest potential: An African American school community in the segregated South.* Chapel Hill, NC: The University of North Carolina Press.

Siddle Walker, V. (2001). African American teacher in the South: 1940–1960. *American Educational Research Journal, 38*(4), 751–779.

Skiba, R. J., Michael, R. S., Nardo, A. C. & Peterson, R. L. (2002). The color of discipline: Sources of racial and gender disproportionality in school punishment. *The Urban Review, 34*, 317–342.

Smith, C. (2021). *How the word is passed: A reckoning with the history of slavery across America.* Little, Brown, & Company.

Smith, P. (2020). "How does a Black person speak English?": Beyond American language norms. *American Educational Research Journal, 57*(1), 106–147.

Souto-Manning, M. (2021). Bridging the teacher education debt: A matter of justice. *Journal of Literacy Research, 53*(4), 588–600.

Sperry, D. E., Sperry, L. L. & Miller, P. J. (2019). Reexamining the verbal environments of children from different socioeconomic backgrounds. *Child Development, 90*(4), 1303–1318.

Stevens, L. P. & Bean, T. W. (2007). *Critical literacy: Context, research, and practice in the K–12 classroom.* SAGE Publications, Inc.

Street, B. (1984). *Literacy in theory and practice.* Cambridge University Press.

Stubbs, T. (2018). *Masters of violence: The plantation overseers of eighteenth-century Virginia, South Carolina, and Georgia (the Carolina Lowcountry and the Atlantic world).* University of South Carolina Press.

Tatum, A. W. (2009). *Reading for the life: (Re)building textual lineages of African American males.* Heinemann.

Tatum, A. W. (2014). Orienting African American male adolescents toward meaningful exchanges with texts. *Journal of Education, 94*(1), 35–47.

Thompkins-Bigelow, J. (2020). *Your name is a song.* The Innovation Press.

U.N. Climate Change. (December 10, 2018). *Greta Thunberg at COP24: "You are never too small to make a difference."* [Video]. https://www.youtube.com/watch?v=CAJuX7xed8o

U.S. Department of Education (n.d.). *Academic performance outcomes for English Learners.* Retrieved from https://www2.ed.gov/datastory/el-outcomes/index.html#one

Valenzuela, A. (1999). *Subtractive schooling: U.S.–Mexican youth and the politics of caring.* State University of New York Press.

Valenzuela, A. (Ed.). (2016). *Growing critically conscious teachers: A social justice curriculum for educators of Latino/a youth.* Teachers College Press.

Vandiver, B. J., Fhagen-Smith, P. E., Cokley, K. O., Cross Jr., W. E. & Worrell, F. C. (2001). Cross's nigrescence model: From theory to scale to theory. *Journal of Multicultural Counseling and Development, 29*(3), 174–200.

Vasquez, V. (2003). *Getting beyond "I like the book": Creating space for critical literacy in K–6 classrooms.* International Reading Association.

Vasquez, V. (2004). *Negotiating critical literacies with young children.* Lawrence Erlbaum.

Vile, J. (2022, November 22). *Stop W.O.K.E. Act (Florida) (2022).* The First Amendment Encyclopedia. https://mtsu.edu/first-amendment/article/2167/stop-w-o-k-e-act-florida

Vygotsky, L. (1978). *Mind in society: The development of high psychological processes.* Harvard University Press.

Wegrzyn, K. M. (2022). Opening up spaces to ask "Why?": Children discussing race and racism. (29992366) [Doctoral Dissertation, The University of Georgia]. ProQuest Dissertations & Thesis Global. https://ezproxy.sju.edu/login?url=https://www.proquest.com/dissertations-theses/opening-up-spaces-ask-why-children-discussing/docview/2773025053/se-2?accountid=14071

Wells, M. S., Morrison, J. D. & López-Robertson, J. (2022). Building critical reading and critical literacy with picturebook analysis. *The Reading Teacher, 76*(2), 191–200.

Wenger-Trayner, E. & Wenger-Trayner, B. (2015). *Introduction to communities of practice: A brief overview of the concept and its uses.* Retrieved from https://www.wenger-trayner.com/wp-content/uploads/2022/06/15-06-Brief-introduction-to-communities-of-practice.pdf

Wetzel, M. (2020). Disrupting race-evasive practices in literacy teacher education: Reflections on research and implications for policy. *Language Arts, 97*(5), 306–316.

Wharton-McDonald, R., Rankin, J. & Mistretta, J. (1997). Effective primary-grades literacy instruction equals balanced literacy instruction. *The Reading Teacher, 50*(6), 518.

Whipp, J. L. (2014). Developing caring with political clarity in high-poverty schools. In *American Educational Research Association Conference, 2014.* American Educational Research Association.

Whipp, J. L. (2016). Factors supporting teachers who practice critical care in urban schools. In *American Educational Research Association Poster Session, 2016.* American Educational Research Association.

Wilkerson, I. (2011). *The warmth of other suns: The epic story of America's great migration.* Vintage.

Williams, P. (1987). Spirit-murdering the messenger: The discourse of fingerpointing as the law's response to racism. *University of Miami Law Review, 42*(1), 127–157.

Williams-Garcia, R. (2011). *One crazy summer.* Thorndike Press Large Print.

Willis, A. I. (2019). Race, response to intervention, and reading research. *Journal of Literacy Research, 51*(4), 394–419.

Winfield, L. F. (1986). Teacher beliefs toward academically at risk students in inner urban schools. *The Urban Review, 18*(4), 253–268.

Wolff, R. D. (2016). How capitalism and racism support each other. Truthout. https://bannekerinstitute.fas.harvard.edu/files/bannekerinstitute/files/how_capitalism_and_racism_support_each_other.pdf

Wood, A. L. (2011). *Lynching and spectacle: Witnessing racial violence in America, 1890–1940*. The University of North Carolina Press.

Wright, B. L. & Counsell, S. L. (2018). *The brilliance of Black boys: Cultivating school success in the early grades*. Teachers College Press.

Wright, Z. (2022). *Dismantling a broken system: Actions to bridge the opportunity, equity, and justice gap in American education*. Solution Tree Press.

Yosso, T. J. (2005). Whose culture has capital?: A Critical Race Theory discussion of community cultural wealth. *Race, Ethnicity, and Education, 8*(1), 69–91.

Zeichner, K. M. (2009). *Teacher education and the struggle for social justice*. Routledge.

Index

About the Authors

Althier M. Lazar is a professor in the Teacher Education Department at Saint Joseph's University in Philadelphia. Her research focuses on understanding the ways teacher candidates acquire the dispositions and skills needed to see and nurture children's literate development. She has authored, coauthored, and edited several books, including *Culturally Sustaining Literacy Pedagogies: Honoring Students' Heritages, Literacies, and Languages* (2022), *Schools of Promise for Multilingual Students* (2018), *New Teachers in Urban Schools: Journeys Toward Social Equity Teaching* (2016), and *Bridging Literacy and Equity: The Essential Guide to Social Equity Teaching* (2012). She has also published numerous articles and book chapters on the topics of teacher growth and literacy teaching for social equity. Dr. Lazar received her PhD from the University of Pennsylvania.

Kaitlin K. Moran is an assistant professor in the Teacher Education Department at Saint Joseph's University in Philadelphia. Her research focuses broadly on improving outcomes for children and families through community-engaged, social-justice–centered scholarship. The lines of inquiry that she explores include pre-service teachers' and practicing teachers' advocacy orientations, early intervention and early childhood special education systems, and high-quality early childhood education and school programming. She has published articles on these lines of inquiry in journals such as *Urban Education*, *Topics in Early Childhood Special Education*, and the *Journal of Early Intervention*. *Connecting Equity, Literacy, and Language: Pathways Toward Advocacy-Focused Teaching* is her first book. Dr. Moran received her PhD from Temple University.

Shoshanna Edwards-Alexander is a clinical assistant professor of social work in the Department of Educational Leadership and Counseling at Saint Joseph's University in Philadelphia. Her research focuses on understanding the relationship between intersectionality and equity within organizations. She is also a diversity, equit,y and inclusion (DEI) strategist who leads seminars, designs and facilitates training programs, and evaluates how inclusive workplace spaces are. Dr. Edwards-Alexander is a licensed clinician, and she received her EdD from Saint Joseph's University.

LANGUAGE AND LITERACY SERIES

Connecting Equity, Literacy, and Language: Pathways Toward Advocacy-Focused Teaching
ALTHIER M. LAZAR, KAITLIN K. MORAN, & SHOSHANNA EDWARDS-ALEXANDER

Writing Instruction for Success in College and in the Workplace
CHARLES A. MACARTHUR & ZOI A. PHILIPPAKOS

Black Immigrant Literacies: Intersections of Race, Language, and Culture in the Classroom
PATRIANN SMITH

Teens Choosing to Read: Fostering Social, Emotional, and Intellectual Growth Through Books
GAY IVEY & PETER JOHNSTON

Critical Encounters in Secondary English: Teaching Literary Theory to Adolescents, 4th Edition
DEBORAH APPLEMAN

Reading With Purpose: Selecting and Using Children's Literature for Inquiry and Engagement
ERIKA THULIN DAWES, KATIE EGAN CUNNINGHAM, GRACE ENRIQUEZ, & MARY ANN CAPPIELLO

Core Practices for Teaching Multilingual Students: Humanizing Pedagogies for Equity
MEGAN MADIGAN PEERCY, JOHANNA M. TIGERT, & DAISY E. FREDRICKS

Bringing Sports Culture to the English Classroom: An Interest-Driven Approach to Literacy Instruction
LUKE RODESILER

Culturally Sustaining Literacy Pedagogies: Honoring Students' Heritages, Literacies, and Languages
SUSAN CHAMBERS CANTRELL, DORIS WALKER-DALHOUSE, & ALTHIER M. LAZAR, EDS.

Curating a Literacy Life: Student-Centered Learning With Digital Media
WILLIAM KIST

Understanding the Transnational Lives and Literacies of Immigrant Children
JUNGMIN KWON

The Administration and Supervision of Literacy Programs, 6th Edition
SHELLEY B. WEPNER & DIANA J. QUATROCHE, EDS.

Writing the School House Blues: Literacy, Equity, and Belonging in a Child's Early Schooling
ANNE HAAS DYSON

Playing With Language: Improving Elementary Reading Through Metalinguistic Awareness
MARCY ZIPKE

Restorative Literacies: Creating a Community of Care in Schools
DEBORAH L. WOLTER

Compose Our World: Project-Based Learning in Secondary English Language Arts
ALISON G. BOARDMAN, ANTERO GARCIA, BRIDGET DALTON, & JOSEPH L. POLMAN

Digitally Supported Disciplinary Literacy for Diverse K–5 Classrooms
JAMIE COLWELL, AMY HUTCHISON, & LINDSAY WOODWARD

The Reading Turn-Around with Emergent Bilinguals: A Five-Part Framework for Powerful Teaching and Learning (Grades K–6)
AMANDA CLAUDIA WAGER, LANE W. CLARKE, & GRACE ENRIQUEZ

Race, Justice, and Activism in Literacy Instruction
VALERIE KINLOCH, TANJA BURKHARD, & CARLOTTA PENN, EDS.

Letting Go of Literary Whiteness: Antiracist Literature Instruction for White Students
CARLIN BORSHEIM-BLACK & SOPHIA TATIANA SARIGIANIDES

The Vulnerable Heart of Literacy: Centering Trauma as Powerful Pedagogy
ELIZABETH DUTRO

Amplifying the Curriculum: Designing Quality Learning Opportunities for English Learners
AÍDA WALQUI & GEORGE C. BUNCH, EDS.

Arts Integration in Diverse K–5 Classrooms: Cultivating Literacy Skills and Conceptual Understanding
LIANE BROUILLETTE

Translanguaging for Emergent Bilinguals: Inclusive Teaching in the Linguistically Diverse Classroom
DANLING FU, XENIA HADJIOANNOU, & XIAODI ZHOU

Before Words: Wordless Picture Books and the Development of Reading in Young Children
JUDITH T. LYSAKER

Seeing the Spectrum: Teaching English Language Arts to Adolescents with Autism
ROBERT ROZEMA

A Think-Aloud Approach to Writing Assessment: Analyzing Process and Product with Adolescent Writers
SARAH W. BECK

"We've Been Doing It Your Way Long Enough": Choosing the Culturally Relevant Classroom
JANICE BAINES, CARMEN TISDALE, & SUSI LONG

Summer Reading: Closing the Rich/Poor Reading Achievement Gap, 2nd Edition
RICHARD L. ALLINGTON & ANNE MCGILL-FRANZEN, EDS.

Educating for Empathy: Literacy Learning and Civic Engagement
NICOLE MIRRA

Preparing English Learners for College and Career: Lessons from Successful High Schools
MARÍA SANTOS ET AL.

Reading the Rainbow: LGBTQ-Inclusive Literacy Instruction in the Elementary Classroom
CAITLIN L. RYAN & JILL M. HERMANN-WILMARTH

Educating Emergent Bilinguals, 2nd Ed.
OFELIA GARCÍA & JO ANNE KLEIFGEN

continued

For volumes in the NCRLL Collection (edited by JoBeth Allen and Donna E. Alvermann), the Practitioners Bookshelf Series (edited by Celia Genishi and Donna E. Alvermann), and other titles in this series, please visit www.tcpress.com

Language and Literacy Series, *continued*

Social Justice Literacies in the English Classroom
Ashley S. Boyd

Remixing Multiliteracies
Frank Serafini & Elisabeth Gee, Eds.

Culturally Sustaining Pedagogies
Django Paris & H. Samy Alim, Eds.

Choice and Agency in the Writing Workshop
Fred L. Hamel

Assessing Writing, Teaching Writers
Mary Ann Smith & Sherry Seale Swain

The Teacher-Writer
Christine M. Dawson

Every Young Child a Reader
Sharan A. Gibson & Barbara Moss

"You Gotta BE the Book," 3rd Ed.
Jeffrey D. Wilhelm

Personal Narrative, Revised
Bronwyn Clare LaMay

Inclusive Literacy Teachings
Lori Helman et al.

The Vocabulary Book, 2nd Ed.
Michael F. Graves

Reading, Writing, and Talk
Mariana Souto-Manning & Jessica Martell

Go Be a Writer!
Candace R. Kuby & Tara Gutshall Rucker

Partnering with Immigrant Communities
Gerald Campano et al.

Teaching Outside the Box but Inside the Standards
Bob Fecho et al., Eds.

Literacy Leadership in Changing Schools
Shelley B. Wepner et al.

Literacy Theory as Practice
Lara J. Handsfield

Literacy and History in Action
Thomas M. McCann et al.

Pose, Wobble, Flow
Antero Garcia & Cindy O'Donnell-Allen

Newsworthy
Ed Madison

Engaging Writers with Multigenre Research Projects
Nancy Mack

Teaching Transnational Youth
Allison Skerrett

Uncommonly Good Ideas
Sandra Murphy & Mary Ann Smith

The One-on-One Reading and Writing Conference
Jennifer Berne & Sophie C. Degener

Transforming Talk into Text
Thomas M. McCann

Educating Literacy Teachers Online
Lane W. Clarke & Susan Watts-Taffee

WHAM! Teaching with Graphic Novels Across the Curriculum
William G. Brozo et al.

Critical Literacy in the Early Childhood Classroom
Candace R. Kuby

Inspiring Dialogue
Mary M. Juzwik et al.

Reading the Visual
Frank Serafini

ReWRITING the Basics
Anne Haas Dyson

Writing Instruction That Works
Arthur N. Applebee et al.

Literacy Playshop
Karen E. Wohlwend

Critical Media Pedagogy
Ernest Morrell et al.

A Search Past Silence
David E. Kirkland

The ELL Writer
Christina Ortmeier-Hooper

Reading in a Participatory Culture
Henry Jenkins et al., Eds.

Teaching Vocabulary to English Language Learners
Michael F. Graves et al.

Bridging Literacy and Equity
Althier M. Lazar et al.

Reading Time
Catherine Compton-Lilly

Interrupting Hate
Mollie V. Blackburn

Playing Their Way into Literacies
Karen E. Wohlwend

Teaching Literacy for Love and Wisdom
Jeffrey D. Wilhelm & Bruce Novak

Urban Literacies
Valerie Kinloch, Ed.

Bedtime Stories and Book Reports
Catherine Compton-Lilly & Stuart Greene, Eds.

Envisioning Knowledge
Judith A. Langer

Envisioning Literature, 2nd Ed.
Judith A. Langer

Artifactual Literacies
Kate Pahl & Jennifer Rowsell

Change Is Gonna Come
Patricia A. Edwards et al.

Harlem on Our Minds
Valerie Kinloch

Children, Language, and Literacy
Celia Genishi & Anne Haas Dyson

Children's Language
Judith Wells Lindfors

Storytime
Lawrence R. Sipe

Connecting Equity, Literacy, and Language

Pathways Toward Advocacy-Focused Teaching

Althier M. Lazar
Kaitlin K. Moran
Shoshanna Edwards-Alexander

Foreword by Delicia Tiera Greene

TEACHERS COLLEGE PRESS
TEACHERS COLLEGE | COLUMBIA UNIVERSITY
NEW YORK AND LONDON

Published by Teachers College Press,® 1234 Amsterdam Avenue, New York, NY 10027

Cover design by Peter Donahue. Cover illustration by digitalgenetics / iStock.

Library of Congress Cataloging-in-Publication Data is available at loc.gov

ISBN 978-0-8077-6874-7 (paper)
ISBN 978-0-8077-6875-4 (hardcover)
ISBN 978-0-8077-8192-0 (ebook)

Printed on acid-free paper
Manufactured in the United States of America

Contents

Foreword

We are amid three pandemics: a medical pandemic due to COVID-19 that has ravaged a nation and impacted the landscape of teaching and learning, a racial pandemic continuously weaved into the fabric of American life that has resulted in Black lives lost at the hands of police-state violence, and an instructional pandemic that has banned Critical Race Theory (CRT) and related concepts from being taught in public and charter schools. These tumultuous times continue to call for teacher educators and teacher education programs to prepare teacher candidates to counter systems designed to marginalize Black and Brown students.

Culturally sustaining pedagogy has been central in countering oppressive learning environments and centering the literate traditions, linguistic nuances, and cultural identities of Black and Brown children; however, these teaching practices have been implemented without accounting for how teacher candidates' perspectives, ideologies, and dispositions influence the degree to which the pedagogy is transformative for Black and Brown children. To fully embrace culturally sustaining pedagogy, teacher educators must guide teacher candidates in engaging in internal work that calls for them to reckon with their perspectives and biases rooted in their power, privilege, and positionalities. Dr. Yolanda Sealey-Ruiz (2021) identifies the internal work paramount in teacher practice as the "archaeology of the self." Like the work of an archaeologist, this entails an excavation process in which teacher candidates engage in introspection to reflect and analyze their preconceived notions about children and families in their school communities.

We (the authors of this book and I) teach predominantly white teacher candidates. The national demographic trends in the teaching force (84%) are comprised of predominantly white, female, monolingual students in their early 20s to early 30s who typically come from rural or suburban working-class communities (U. S. Department of Education, 2016). Like Lazar et al.'s teachers, my teacher candidates often go on to work in school districts that serve Black children while lacking cultural awareness and understanding of their students' backgrounds. Further, school districts often do not facilitate initiatives designed to support teacher candidates in the internal work necessary to be culturally aware and conscious, resulting in White teachers often framing Black and Brown children with deficit lenses.

Given this reality, teacher education programs are fertile ground for facilitating teacher candidates' reflexive practice. In my adolescent literature course, teacher candidates' reflexive practice is a primary focus, while approaches to teaching literature texts in their literacy classroom are the secondary focus. Teacher candidates' approaches to teaching literature texts in their literacy classrooms are shaped by the degree to which one engages in internal work. The course prompts teacher candidates to think about their reader identities. Who are you as a reader? How do your intersecting personal and professional identities influence how you interpret the text? What tensions, if any, did you grapple with while reading this text, and what contributed to these tensions? The course also prompts teacher candidates to think about their teacher identities. How might you introduce and teach this text in your classroom? What concerns might you have, if any, in teaching this text? How might you introduce this text to a population that is racially, socioeconomically, and culturally different from the characters in the text?

The work starts with us. We are not passive inhabitants of a system that exists without our input. To this point, Lazar et al. reveal that "we are the system," and we either confirm or counter the injustices that are part of that system. I often inform my students that failed systems are not abstract entities in a distant land. They are in our backyard. We either conform to them or actively resist them. Teacher candidates have full agency and participation in the system and must be moved to interrogate positionality, power, and privilege to fully engage in equity work. Lazar et al. offer a window into teacher candidates' experiences through vignettes that illustrate the complexity of their journey. Further, the authors depict the urgency of now as they draw linkages across teacher candidates' internal work and the climate and conditions prevalent for Black and Brown children in school spaces. The authors call on us to engage in the difficult and vital work necessary to dismantle systems that fail Black and Brown children. Lazar et al. guide us in answering the following: *How do we engage in internal work to ensure that we enact consciousness and awareness that affords Black and Brown children liberatory learning environments?* It is only with a commitment to continuous excavation that teachers can commit fully to an activist, emancipatory pedagogical agenda.

—*Delicia Tiera Greene*

REFERENCES

Sealey-Ruiz, Y. (2021). The critical literacy of race: Toward racial literacy in urban teacher education. In H. R. Milner IV & K. Lomotey (Eds.), *Handbook of urban education* (pp. 281–295). Routledge.

U. S. Department of Education. (2016). *The state of racial diversity in the educator workforce.* https://www2.ed.gov/rschstat/eval/highered/racial-diversity/state-racial-diversity-workforce.pdf

Acknowledgments

We are indebted to the teachers who have generously shared their experiences and insights with us to make this book possible. Laura, Cecilia, Andrea, Jennifer, Kristin and Burton have made this work real and, in many respects, reproducible. Their talents and dedication to their students are inspiring and fill us with hope for what is possible for all students.

Thanks to the many wise folks at Teachers College Press who have put a lot of thought and energy into this project. To Emily Spangler – thank you for seeing the merits of our initial proposal. Your encouraging words and clear communication helped us to keep the project moving forward. We thank the reviewers who read the earliest drafts of this book and who helped us bring coherence to our initial arguments and stories. Another shout out goes to the editorial staff at Westchester Publishing Services who worked to polish up the final manuscript. Jitendra Kumar, we are grateful for your attention to detail.

On our campus, we would like to thank Michele Donnelly, our graduate assistant, who managed the citations and references for this book. We relied on her keen eye and excellent organizational skills we produced this manuscript.

Finally, each of us is grateful for being able to work with such dedicated co-writers/colleagues, who, despite the intensity of our jobs, believed in this finished this book. We leaned on each other while making hundreds of decisions about the content and style of this book. It was a great collaboration.

Introduction

> We come to work when we don't feel like it, and we're listening to policy that doesn't make sense, and we teach anyway. We teach anyway because that's what we do.
>
> —Rita Pierson (2013)

OUR PURPOSE

Book bans, hotlines to report divisive teaching, Critical Race Theory on the ballot, "Don't Say Gay," arming teachers with guns . . . the list goes on. While all of these issues play out in the news, a more fundamental problem with schooling exists. Too many students are disconnected from school, limiting their ability to be the readers and writers they could be. We are especially failing students from culturally and linguistically marginalized communities. There are many reasons for this, including everything from inequitable school funding to systemic gaps in teacher preparation. What we aim to do is focus on the teacher education gap (Love, 2019), or programs that "perpetuate the stereotyping and myth-making targeted at dark children and their communities" (p. 127), and specifically, the literacy teacher education gap, and offer concepts, teaching frameworks, and teacher profiles to show how we, as educators, can move the needle on that gap.

No packaged one-size-fits-all literacy program will help us see and nurture students' fullest literacy potential. No standardized literacy tests will help kids fall in love with the written word. We can't shrug and say it's the system's fault that kids are turned off to school literacy learning, as if we can pin the problem on some imagined group of school district bureaucrats. As educators working in the sphere of literacy/language studies, we must turn to ourselves and do the kinds of self-education work that will allow us to create loving, welcoming literacy communities inside our schools. We must do the work that will help us dismantle racist ideas and structures from the inside out, in our classrooms, schools, and districts. *We educators are the system*. It's time we reclaim the narrative about us and our work.

There are plenty of books and articles that show what culturally centered literacy classrooms look like. They show teachers who are committed to students and students' communities, have acquired a certain level of competency in the profession, and routinely connect literacy teaching with issues of equity. Often hidden from our view is how these teachers got to be this way. How did they come to grow in their commitment to students and communities? How did they come to notice and dismantle inequitable literacy teaching practices? *How did they come to be such advocacy-oriented teachers?*

We are especially intrigued by these teachers because so many educators in our circles do not have opportunities to study or reflect on the complex interrelationships between equity and literacy. Most of us have not had opportunities to excavate our racial understandings and discover how this critical self-work translates to our classrooms. Further, many teachers we know are afraid to instigate change in their schools. They are worried they will be demoted, reassigned, or fired for speaking out. We are aware that these are politically divisive times. Some states are trying to ban all classroom discussions about racial injustice, sexuality, and gender identity. The thing to remember is that the numbers are on our side. We need more good educators who can support each other's advocacy efforts. There is a large coalition of educators showing up to work every day committed to advocacy-focused teaching because that's what we do, as Rita Pierson (2013) said. This work is possible and there is a path forward for every educator who wants to engage in it.

This book does not contain magical encyclopedic capabilities, but it does offer an "on ramp," if you will. What we aim to do is take the ideas of advocacy teaching and clarify what they mean in the context of literacy learning. Current models of culturally and historically responsive teaching (Ladson-Billings, 2009; Muhammad, 2020; Paris, 2012) rest on the assumption that teachers have engaged in the self-work needed to enact these frameworks. This is not always the case. Many new and experienced teachers do not have opportunities to relate literacy to concepts like racial injustice or white supremacy. Equity issues are largely disconnected from literacy teaching in teacher education programs and professional development offerings. The overwhelming focus of literacy education curricula is pedagogy, leaving concepts of equity, literacy, and language disconnected in the minds of many educators. As a result, many good-faith efforts to bring culturally sustaining pedagogies to classrooms remain superficial and whitewashed (Ladson-Billings & Dixson, 2022), with partial efforts that include adding more multicultural books to our classroom libraries or having students write about their home experiences. Without constructing deep and ongoing understandings about critical issues like systemic racism, real advocacy work cannot happen. Without watchful and critical teacher advocates, educational inequities such as undifferentiated literacy instruction will continue to undermine many students' learning opportunities.

This short book will raise your consciousness about issues of equity as it relates to literacy teaching and learning, but its relative brevity means that you'll want to study several concepts independently or with your colleagues. Future and practicing educators can be overwhelmed trying to match the realities they face daily with the theoretical, pedagogical, and empirical works that scholars spend their entire careers developing and studying. This book introduces you to some important conceptual and practical anchors to build from so you can continue your journey toward becoming an advocacy-focused literacy teacher. To that end, we also provide key resources after each chapter to give you both direction and additional support. We hope that you see this book as a place you can come to, and come back to, to continue to deepen your understanding of the issues and to find inspiration, hope, and community.

Did you notice that we don't include a section on literacy or language teaching methods in this book? After all, don't teachers need to develop pedagogical expertise in order to create readers, writers, and thinkers? Of course they do. The professional field, however, is filled with excellent books and articles on literacy/language instruction and assessment. With all the methodological knowledge out there, you'd think we would have eliminated the problem of literacy failure by now. We haven't. That's why we need educators who not only bring their pedagogical knowledge and skills to classrooms, but also bring their caring, loving selves to the job. They need to continually learn about the sociocultural, sociopolitical, and sociohistorical nature of their work. They need to construct some fundamental understandings about the nature of educational equity and how it relates to literacy learning and teaching. We provide many of these beyond-pedagogy pieces in this book.

STRUCTURE OF THE BOOK

We are three teacher educators who are committed to helping educators stand in solidarity with students of color and their caregivers, see the limitless potential of students, and deliver enriched, critical, and culturally centered teaching—all characteristics of advocacy-oriented teachers. Our frame of reference is working with teachers and teacher candidates in and around the city of Philadelphia. We bring over 60 years of experience to this project and frequently reflect on how these experiences have helped us grow as people and as educators. We consider ourselves to be on the journey with you. Your realities and perspectives may either resonate with ours or be different depending on your own political, social, economic, and geographic context. Regardless of context, many of the concepts and challenges we discuss are universal, or are becoming universal, in our profession. The incredible educators we will introduce you to may work locally, but we see their approaches as replicable and offering value to educators teaching in all kinds of classroom contexts. We hope that you are as inspired by them, and their work, as we are.

We begin in Chapter 1 by examining the central problem of students' disconnection with school through the experience of Ta-Nehisi Coates (2015), the celebrated author of the book *Between the World and Me,* who writes about being metaphorically shackled by Baltimore's public schools, in relation to the teacher education gap. In Chapter 2, we discuss the need to examine ourselves and the communities where we teach, as part of developing the racial and cultural understandings needed to advocate for students. In Chapter 3 we look at particular school and classroom inequities that have become so normalized in schools, including standardized testing, literacy teaching routines and structures, and deficit-laced language about students and families. In Chapter 4, we examine issues of culture, race, and intersectionality and how these and other related constructs link with literacy learning and teaching. Next, we discuss literacies and languages as cultural practices in Chapter 5, and the need to be vigilant in dismantling the linguistic violence that occurs when students' languages are delegitimized. In Chapter 6, we describe culturally centered teaching frameworks and include specific examples of literacy practice by local educators. This conversation continues in Chapter 7 as we unpack how we can move toward critical teaching and advocacy work, again finding inspiration from local educators. We finish the book with a look at next steps for how we might continue to learn and grow as literacy advocacy teachers in Chapter 8.

Every one of the topics in this book is worthy of intensive inquiry, and the empirical research that holds it up. The issue is, however, that the profession is under siege and there is no time for *more* demanding, rigorous, exhaustive work. We also recognize that this is a profession that has been inundated with bad news. The realities are . . . real, but it's not all doom and gloom. There is plenty of work to be done, but there are really incredible people taking up the challenge—and you can too. To support you, we want to synthesize the information that is out there, overview the work that has been done, personalize and contextualize these frameworks and pedagogies and big questions, and ultimately empower you to know that in the face of significant challenges, what we know and what we do, inside and outside of our classrooms, matters greatly to those in them. This book is a book of shared experiences written by educators for educators, current and future. Individually, and as co-authors, we believe in the infinite potential of all students, and we are advocating for the full inclusion of all students in our classrooms.

WHO WE ARE

Althier M. Lazar is a white cisgender woman who has worked with many talented teachers and students within the mostly Black and Latinx communities of West and North Philadelphia for almost 3 decades. She has also worked to cultivate teacher candidates' capacity orientations of the students and families in these communities. This journey started with her own deep dive into how whiteness has operated in her history and work (Lazar, 2004), and it has transpired over many years of learning and writing about intersections between race, culture, literacy, and language. She lives with an awareness that she may perpetuate settler colonialism/white supremacist ideas through her words and deeds and so is continually interrogating her work from these perspectives.

Kaitlin K. Moran is a Spanish-speaking white cisgender woman who has worked with families in urban communities as a bilingual educator and researcher for nearly 2 decades. In this work, she has experienced the richness and vibrancy present in marginalized communities and is deeply committed to guiding preservice and current teachers to do the same. Kaitlin is on a lifelong journey as she continues to develop her awareness of race and culture, which includes being aware of her whiteness, accepting her role in perpetuating racism, and remaining committed to abandoning white entitlement.

Shoshanna Edwards-Alexander is a Black cisgender woman who has worked as a diversity educator/consultant and licensed social work clinician in Philadelphia for over 20 years. Reflecting on her own academic journey as a woman of color who was primarily educated at predominantly white institutions (PWIs), Shoshanna's academic focus has been centered around multicultural competency development. This is particularly important in her teaching practice, as she frequently works with preservice teachers entering primarily urban school districts. Her work includes developing teaching practices that support cross-cultural interactions and foster inclusive learning environments.

We teach at Saint Joseph's University, a faith-based Catholic-affiliated university with a largely white population of students and teacher candidates; students of color make up about 20% of our undergraduate student body and 55% of our graduate population. Our university is located at the western edge of Philadelphia, on a route that separates the largely Black working- and middle-class community of Overbrook in Philadelphia from the primarily white, middle-class and affluent township of Lower Merion. The differences in schooling opportunities between these populations is stark, with lower resourced schools on the Philadelphia side. Our teacher candidates intern at schools on both sides of the avenue and our graduate students often teach, or have teaching experiences, in both fully resourced and under-resourced settings so that they see the effects of the racial divide up close. We've sculpted the teacher education curriculum in ways that help all of our students notice and name educational inequities that are clearly visible from our location.

We come to this work with different perspectives and experiences, but with the same goal: to support educators in recognizing and nurturing students' limitless literate potential. We weave our personal and professional experiences into this writing, including the ways we have been students, teachers, coaches, and observers in schools. We mesh our stories with the theoretical positions and research findings that speak to equity literacy teaching. We wanted to deliver these ideas in an informal and comfortable style, with questions, and wonderings, and our own bursts of joy or outrage. This should be down-to-earth talk that does not belong to the academy, but to everybody. We also lean on an incredible body of educators, some new and others seasoned, whose identities are as diverse as their students. We know these teachers, we have spent time in their classrooms, we have witnessed their commitment, and we are humbled by their generosity in allowing us to share with you their triumphs, their challenges, and the many, many ways they are living and breathing advocacy-focused literacy teaching.

For your part, we ask that you engage thoughtfully with the ideas in this book. Wrestle with them and talk back to them. We pack a lot of big ideas into this short book and know that each idea deserves more thoughtful study. We hope that you use the book as your on-ramp, an invitation to continue down the road and explore concepts in much greater depth. We hope that you follow the experts that we profile in this book and read their scholarship or listen to their TED talks. You might follow them on Instagram, watch their webinars, subscribe to their blogs, and organize your own professional learning communities to discover and reflect on their work. Combining equity discoveries with your knowledge of pedagogy will take you far toward being the advocacy teacher that is within you. So, let's begin.

CHAPTER 1

A Need for Advocacy-Focused Literacy Educators

> **The streets were not my only problem. If the streets shackled my right leg, the schools shackled my left. Fail to comprehend the streets and you gave up your body now. But fail to comprehend the schools and you gave up your body later. I suffered at the hands of both but I resent the schools more.**
>
> —Ta-Nehisi Coates (2015)

A RECKONING

In his book *Between the World and Me* (2015), Ta-Nehisi Coates writes to his son about how the public school system failed him. His experience is one that is felt by far too many culturally, racially, and/or linguistically marginalized students. From unequal school funding to students' misidentification with schools, to teachers who are ill-prepared to educate everyone's child—these and other elements of schooling deprive many students of a decent education. As a result, we have failed to secure a core educational goal to help all students realize their fullest literate potential. We educators, however, can confront these conditions. We know this because we've seen it. In this book, we will share the voices of teachers who are making literacy classrooms equitable, joyful, and loving places for literacy learning. We will also share some key concepts that ground these teachers' understandings and competencies. As you read, we invite you to connect, reflect, and envision what advocacy-focused literacy teaching might look like for you.

Let's begin by looking at the inequitable landscape of schooling and literacy learning. Vast funding discrepancies in public education mean that schools in highly economically stressed communities receive fewer material resources, experienced teachers and staff, and curriculum offerings than do schools in more affluent communities. Neo-liberal views about educating students for the marketplace have influenced the prevalence of high-stakes tests that de-professionalize teachers and narrow the curriculum, primarily in schools with low achievement rates. These schools are more apt to use prepackaged "teacher proof" literacy programs, standardized tests, computerized learning systems, and other curricula materials that fail to account for the cultural capital and diverse literacies that youth in marginalized communities bring to school. Years spent filling out meaningless worksheets, preparing for standardized tests, and sitting in classrooms with irrelevant and uninspired teaching can chisel away at the mind, little by little, until students' curiosity and their interest in school is beaten down. Further, minoritized students are often criminalized within school buildings by metal detectors installed in school entrances, police cruisers camped outside of school doors, and proto-military forms of discipline that strip kids of their humanity (e.g., Coates, 2015; Delpit, 2019; Kozol, 2006; Love, 2019; Wright, 2022).

In her book *We Want to Do More Than Survive* (2019), Bettina Love writes about how schools function to "feed the school-to-prison pipeline that targets dark children" (p. 31). She details how physical and verbal assaults, harsh suspension policies, high-stakes state tests, and teachers who fail to see children's highest potential are some of the elements that converge to *spirit-murder* students of color. Spirit-murdering is a term first coined by legal scholar Patricia Williams (1987) to capture the ways that laws are used to oppress and crush the spirits of people of color. Schools do the same to students. Some educational inequities are overt. We know them when we see them and our teacher candidates do as well. One teacher candidate in Shoshanna's class shared her observations about two teachers who seemed to be giving up on students:

> One of the teachers just puts on a video and sits at his desk reading the paper. Another (teacher) said I could work with a group of students she called "the troublemakers," while she taught a handful of students. How are these kids going to learn in this type of environment?

There's no other way to read this observational note. Some students in this school setting are neglected, while others are stigmatized. These are overt forms of spirit-murdering. While we are very concerned about these systemic ways of separating students from school, we will focus on the more subtle types of spirit-murdering that often go unnoticed in literacy classrooms. Undifferentiated literacy instruction, keeping kids in the same reading groups all year long, having students answer low-level recall questions, insisting that they use the "correct" language when they speak, teaching reading from a script, using culturally irrelevant books and materials, aiming for basic and proficient performance instead of advanced, having students respond to writing prompts without showing them how to write—all of these all-to-common practices slowly but steadily contribute to the spirit-murdering that goes on in the literacy classroom. Well-intentioned teachers may not see any of these activities as spirit-murdering because they are so normalized in classrooms, but they are. Adding to these abuses is the way students are denigrated for speaking, behaving, and presenting in ways that do not correspond with dominant white norms. Education scholar Richard Milner reflects:

> Most of the important dimensions of my being had to be checked at the door when I arrived at school. I was expected to become a much different Rich when I walked into the classroom. I was expected to become, what felt to me, a much whiter person. Specifically, my teachers (Black, Brown, and white) expected and demanded I check my language, how I dressed, what I listened to, all at the entrance of the school. And so for me—I wore a mask that eventually meant I grinned and lied to satisfy teachers (and to an extent, a schooling system that was not meant for me) who tried to cultivate my identity into something very different from what I enjoyed, connected to, and yearned for." (Milner, 2017, p. 75)

While literacy classrooms can be sites of spirit-murdering, they can also be sites of identification, liberation, and joy. Further in his narrative, Milner discusses how the language arts curriculum offered him a space to reflect on and make sense of his own life and world. Milner's insights point to the potential of literacy educators to connect with kids who find themselves culturally disenfranchised by schools.

This is the point of this book: Literacy educators have a special role to play in not only abolishing the spirit-murdering that goes on in classrooms, but creating a space of deep meaning and joy around using and thinking about languages and literacies. In our years working directly with apprentice and experienced teachers, we have come to realize that we can get to this place by developing *commitments* to students and their communities and *competencies* as advocacy-focused literacy teachers. Building competencies in advocacy-focused literacy teaching is complicated by the reality that most literacy curricula and professional development programs focus almost exclusively on literacy methodologies, allowing little room to connect equity issues to literacy teaching practice. This means that teacher candidates and teachers often have to make these connections on their own or by following like-minded educators who are profiled in professional texts or social media. This may be your experience, or it may not, but whatever your path, we encourage you to think about centering these commitments and competencies.

Equity-mindedness means having a constant, wide-eyed state of awareness about the ways students are advantaged/disadvantaged by their racial affiliation, language, gender, religion, citizenship, sexual orientation, and other identity markers. It means examining how issues of equity/inequity relate to students' literacy development and providing the needed supports to help students realize their fullest literacy potential. A knowledge of equity propels us to understand ourselves, our biases, our literacy histories, and our moral obligations. It moves us to know students, their families, and their communities and to honor students' literacies, languages, and knowledge traditions in the classroom. This awareness helps us notice, call out, and dismantle the practices and policies that prevent students from realizing their fullest literacy potential. These ways of being and doing fit with Bettina Love's (2019) notion of *abolitionist* teaching:

> Abolitionist teaching is the practice of working in solidarity with communities of color while drawing on the imagination, creativity, refusal, (re)membering, visionary thinking, healing, rebellious spirit, boldness, determination, and subversiveness of abolitionists to eradicate injustice in and outside of schools. (p. 2)

Abolitionist teaching says that the most formative school years should be productively and joyfully spent in the company of teachers who love them, care for them, respect them, and who are willing and able to resist and eliminate the elements that undermine students' fullest potential. We would add that abolitionist teachers are *instructionally agile* and are willing to disrupt normative ways of thinking about what gets taught (curriculum) and how it gets taught (instruction) (Milner, 2020). At the center of abolitionist teaching is the ethical question of how we matter to ourselves, to our students, and to our students' communities.

Right now you might be reading this thinking: *Sure, I'm down with that but I don't know how!* Or perhaps you're thinking: *I know, and I'm trying, but it's overwhelming in this climate!* While most of us go into teaching thinking that we matter and that our students matter, we may not be prepared to work as advocacy-focused teachers or if we have been, we may be experiencing burnout or frustration in trying to sustain these efforts. Either way, you are not alone. New or seasoned, we can often feel powerless to take on entrenched school policies. We ask: *Can we really question the way writing is taught in this school? Can we work with colleagues to disrupt the district's reading program so it better meets our students' literacy needs? Can we take a stand against the deficit-oriented ways that students and their families are described?* If we notice inequities but do not act to challenge them, we will become part of the problem, as reflected by Coates' thoughts about the suffering he endured through his schooling experiences. *We educators*—teachers, teacher educators, teacher candidates, those in administration, those in support roles, those who are supporting children in other capacities—cannot be complicit in the spirit-murdering that happens in schools and in literacy classrooms. We believe that advocacy work is not just possible for educators, but integral to one's role as a literacy professional.

What does it take for us to advocate for children in the literacy classroom? Shouldn't we focus on learning more or better teaching methods?

Teaching well can be practiced and learned, but no matter how many teaching skills and strategies we acquire, we will never be able to teach kids to read if we don't respect them, their families, their communities, or their heritage.

Here is the reckoning: We might think we respect all kids. We think we see every student's literacy potential. We say these things and think we believe them. We must, however, acknowledge that all of us—all of us—have been shaped by racist policies and ideas that are endemic to life in the United States and other parts of the world (Kendi, 2019). Many of us, not all, but many enter the field of education with racial biases and large gaps in our understanding about students and communities. If this is true for you, it's critical to understand that we bring these biases and knowledge gaps to our work because systems of teacher education, accreditation, and licensure, purportedly designed to educate us, have often fallen short in this regard—an issue we will discuss in the next section. We fully believe, however, that whatever your experiences have been, whatever your preparation has looked like, you can do this work. We have seen how the ideas in this book have shaped the perceptions and actions of many educators we know, and it can happen for you. For now, let's take a moment to consider how spirit-murdering might be working to undermine students' literacy learning in the schools that you know best.

Pause and Reflect

1. Think about the ways that spirit-murdering could be happening at your school or the schools you have visited. Take a moment to list these ways. How might these ways interfere with students' literacy learning?
2. What attributes do you think you bring to the goal of seeing and nurturing all students' fullest literacy capacities? What challenges do you see for yourself in meeting this goal?

THE TEACHER EDUCATION GAP

Teacher education and professional development offerings have left many of us adrift without sufficient sociocultural, sociopolitical, and sociohistorical knowledge. Gutiérrez and Lee (2009) have charged that teacher preparation programs typically do not help teacher candidates understand how to address social justice goals, nor do they do enough to challenge teacher candidates' racial biases. These programs have been called out for their inability to address issues when preparing teachers to work with students of color (Alvarez & Milner, 2018; Edwards et al., 2010) or discuss issues of race and racial violence (Milner, 2020). With school districts and teacher education programs focusing on testing, Common Core Standards, and elements of "best practices," future and practicing teachers have few professional spaces in which to become racially and socioculturally, politically, historically literate.

At our university, we have tried hard to ensure that the graduates of our teacher education program develop antiracist, advocacy dispositions but this is difficult and ongoing work. Over the last 10 years, we have integrated several critical consciousness-raising topics into our curricula such as systemic racism, white privilege, meritocracy, and literacies and languages as cultural practices. Only relatively recently have we also made sure to address white supremacy, settler colonialism, raciolinguistics, and intersectionality. You may be nodding your head, familiar with some of these concepts, but if you are not, it is not your fault and you might be wondering why this is the case. Being unfamiliar with these concepts means that your teacher education and professional development programs have failed to help you become socioculturally literate, and the accreditation and licensing bodies in your state have let teacher education programs off the hook for being accountable to your professional growth. You are not alone. Too many graduates of teacher education programs are getting licensed to teach without the mindsets needed to serve culturally marginalized students well. Bettina Love (2019) aptly calls this the "teacher education gap." To this notion we would add the "school leader education gap" which means we really need to be talking about the "educator education gap."

The educator education gap is often evident in teacher candidates' perceptions of students and teaching. More than a decade ago, Anthony Castro (2010) produced a meta-analysis of teacher candidates' understandings about teaching in culturally marginalized communities. He found that while teacher candidates are much more accepting of cultural differences than in decades past, many had not acquired the complex understandings that would prepare them to serve students in minoritized communities because they were blind to the structural and institutional inequalities of schools and society that shape students' access to achievement. Lacking these understandings, Castro noted that future teachers were likely to "blame oppressed peoples for their 'failure' in the system of schooling rather than to recognize the system of failure embedded in institutional practices that disfavors and disenfranchises minority groups" (Castro, 2010, p. 207). Further, while teacher educators have made some progress in helping teachers consider the importance of race-centered discussions with students, many teachers are still uncomfortable about leading these discussions, and most believe their teacher education programs have not prepared them for this work (Milner, 2017).

Many teacher education and professional development programs have not done a good enough job developing teachers' sociocultural and sociopolitical competencies related to literacy studies. Literacy teacher educators become complicit in miseducating teachers about issues of race and culture when the voices of teachers of color are left out (Souto-Manning, 2021). The normalization of whiteness and the mastery of academic English in literacy curricula is not well scrutinized in literacy education courses (Daniels & Varghese, 2020; Wetzel, 2020). This means that you may or may not have had opportunities to develop the dispositions needed to notice and name inequities around literacy teaching, standards, and assessment practices or to offer alternative frameworks and practices that value and build on all students' literacies and languages. It also means that you may not feel prepared to join the disruptive movement that is focused on exposing and challenging white supremacy in the literacy curriculum or in the ways literacy is taught and literate performance is assessed (Milner, 2020).

Gaps in educator education, and particularly literacy education, mean that many teachers tend to see advocacy teaching as something detached from literacy teaching, or something that special brave and selfless teachers do . . . those who have more energy, commitment, experience, or standing. We may think we are being advocates for students by adding some multicultural books to our classroom libraries or inviting students to write about their home experiences. Do these actions inspire kids like Ta-Nehisi Coates to fall in love with books and see school as a place to cultivate a rich literate life? They help, but they are simply not enough. We can, and must, do more.

TEACHER DEVELOPMENT: BUILDING COMMITMENTS AND COMPETENCIES

The kind of work it takes to foster all students' engagement with school requires transformation at the level of teacher *dispositions*. Dispositions are beliefs, understandings, and inclinations about ourselves, students, communities, reflection, inquiry, fairness, and justice and how we might act in accord with these ideas (Schussler, 2006). Beliefs, understandings, and inclinations shape teacher decision-making and actions (Gay, 2010; Milner, 2015). To illustrate, let's look at the case of Shoshanna's aunt, Laura, a teacher who exemplifies what it means to be advocacy-focused.

Laura identifies as Black and teaches in a southern Christian school that serves primarily students of color. Laura is a classic *warm demander* (Kleinfeld, 1975). Warm demanders are teachers who "expect a great deal of their students, convince them of their own brilliance, and help them to reach their potential in a disciplined and structured environment" (Delpit, 2013). Says Laura: *The running joke is "You know Ms. Laura doesn't play games." When it comes to my classroom my kids know I mean business!*

They also recognize that I really care about their learning, and I want to see them succeed. Laura explains:

> I believe in my students, and (want) them to believe in themselves. A lot of times people give up on our kids . . . they fail them. These kids have the potential, it just takes patience on our part to help them. I know these kids, I've taught their siblings and aunties, I go to church with their grandmothers, we see each other in the grocery stores, they think of me as an extended part of their families. When the parents drop them off the first day of school they'll say Ms. Laura, I'm not worried about [the student]. I know [the student] is in good hands. I show them love but hold them accountable the same way I raised my children. I must because the world is going to hold them accountable. I need them to be prepared. They know that even when I have to have a conversation with them about their behavior or work, it's coming from a place of love.

We emphasize Laura's profound statement: *I show them love but hold them accountable in the same way I raised my children.* She teaches in "a culture of love" (Lewis, 2018), which means that she extends the same aspirations for her students that she has for her own children. And while she sees herself as a member of her students' community, and understands the capital and wealth it possesses, she also acknowledges the political nature of her work and how people *give up on students, but yet hold them accountable.* She is aware that society expects her students to achieve and knows she must fight for her students (because others may not). Laura's devotion to her students' welfare, her eye on the way the world sees and treats her students, and her insider status within her community are all attributes of advocacy-focused teachers. Another attribute is her ability to create a classroom that mirrors students' experiences and heritage, and to draw from students' knowledge traditions to build new learning opportunities. She explains:

> A lot of my kids listen to rap and hip-hop music or R&B. I'll bring in some Billie Holiday, or Stevie Wonder, and show them how their "modern" music is born out of the classics. I've even brought in vinyl records, and old-school 8-track tapes. I'm able to create lessons around these things that also align with our district materials. I keep pictures all over my classroom and plenty of books and other materials that highlight people of color. I do something called "spotlight features" so every month we feature someone and their accomplishments. Most recently, our spotlight was on Cecilia Cruz, a Cuban American singer who reigned for decades as the "Queen of Salsa Music." This is just another opportunity to expose our kids to genres that they might not otherwise get to experience.

When explaining how she adheres to district literacy standards, she indicates that she supplements the reading materials the district uses with resources that reflect students' cultural identities. For instance, when Barack Obama's book, Lessons from My Father, came out, she had students read it instead of the text suggested by the district. According to Laura, upholding students' cultural identities is of paramount importance: *It is important that our children see images and read books that embrace their communities. This gives them a sense of cultural, ethnic, and racial pride that they don't get from the district materials.* By establishing a positive and identity-affirming environment for literacy learning, Laura is able to maintain a laser-sharp focus on literacy achievement, as is evident from this comment:

> I often say my students are teaching me while I'm teaching them. I want them to feel that they can contribute to the lesson plan, the book chapters that we choose, that they can contribute to the assignments we do . . . to everything in our room. This not only helps contribute to enhancing their literacy development, it gives them a sense of pride, and bolsters their self-esteem. It also improves their cognitive abilities and advances critical thinking and problem-solving skills.

Note how Laura shares power with her students by welcoming their ideas about lessons and reading materials. In doing so, she develops students' identities as literacy achievers, as well as their capacities as intellectuals and critical thinkers. Laura also gets families involved in literacy learning routines while scaffolding students' reading instruction. She does this by sending students home with texts that they can read on their own or with their caregivers prior to coming to school. Literacy in Laura's class is not just about reading. She also encourages a wide variety of writing as well as art and creative activities, and students are invited to write stories, poetry, and song lyrics.

In addition, Laura creates a positive learning environment that encourages students to self-regulate their behavior. She gives students daily mantras to live by and to ground their day.

Some examples are "I will practice kindness today," "I am grateful for . . .," I promise to share," and so forth. She takes a few minutes to invite discussion on what these mantras mean to students and how they plan to practice them. When she finds that students are not behaving in accordance with these mantras, she reminds them: *Jake, do you remember our mantra from this morning? It doesn't seem to me that you are following it.* This helps students find accountability for their behavior without yelling at them or penalizing them in front of their peers.

Let's just take a moment to digest what Laura thinks and does. She

1. sees her students as full of promise;
2. recognizes how society may give up on her students, yet will surely hold them accountable;

3. understands that her students' literate identities are preserved when they read texts that reflect their experiences and cultures;
4. is a trusted member of her students' communities;
5. takes full responsibility for teaching her students and prepares them for a world that will judge them (action);
6. welcomes students' contributions to assignments;
7. provides students with a variety of materials and activities that preserve their identities;
8. advances their critical thinking and problem-solving abilities;
9. substitutes district reading materials with more culturally affirming ones while adhering to the district's academic standards; and
10. she loves her students as her own.

All of these thoughts and actions make Laura an advocacy-focused teacher. In drawing from Laura's case, as well as other narratives of advocacy-focused literacy practice, we propose that development toward this type of teaching requires simultaneous focus on moral commitments and acquiring advocacy-focused literacy competencies. Let us reflect on how she and educators like her view their students, themselves, and the world, and how they take action to advance their students' literacy capacities. We can all grow to be our own kind of Laura.

When we encounter teachers like Laura we want to know: *How did she become so invested in her students? How did she come to care so much? How is it possible to develop the kind of moral obligation, desire, and sense of justice that Laura exudes, and then act on these beliefs?* Developing understandings about what we *ought to do* (moral action) that guide what we *choose to do* (ethical agency) requires that we encounter and reflect on "moral dilemmas in the embedded contexts of teaching, learning, schooling, and education" (Diez & Murrell, 2010, p. 13). We experience moral dilemmas first-hand by seeing how students in more affluent, primarily white communities often get richer, more intellectually stimulating, and culturally compatible education than students who live in more economically distressed communities, many of whom are students of color. These encounters are awakenings. They disturb. They needle. They produce anger and discomfort. These rational and visceral responses are moral encounters that become part of the journey toward *caring with political clarity* (Whipp, 2016). Reflecting on these encounters is necessary for building the moral dispositions needed to translate moral thoughts (what you should do) into advocacy-focused actions (what you will or can do). Knowing what to do is a matter of developing competencies as advocacy-focused educators. For this discussion, we turn to the idea of teacher development as a way of growing into a landscape of professional practice.

CONNECTING EQUITY, LITERACY, AND LANGUAGE IN A LANDSCAPE OF PRACTICE

Teachers like Laura turn moral thoughts into advocacy-focused actions through critical and culturally centered teaching practices. How can all teachers develop these teaching competencies? Developing teaching expertise involves engaging in many communities of practice across time—from being a student, to studying about teaching in a university classroom, to participating in a professional development program with colleagues—these are all communities of practice. In these communities, we can imagine what sort of teacher we can become, what we need to know, and what we need to do. It is through involvement in many different communities that we gain expertise across "a landscape of practice" (Wenger-Trayner & Wenger-Trayner, 2015). A "landscape of practice" represents the body of knowledge of a profession, "consisting of a complex system of communities of practice and the boundaries between them" (p. 13). Not only do we engage in various communities of practice, but there are also communities of practice that determine what teachers should know and do, including a community that produces books and scholarly articles about teaching, one that determines accreditation standards at state and national levels, another that decides what subject matter should be taught within a district level, and so forth. Together, these communities establish a "regime of competence" (p. 14) which is the knowledge and practices associated with what teachers should know and do.

Each community of practice jostles to assert control over what constitutes professional competency. In the field of education, some communities agree with what teachers should know and do, some do not. For instance, most communities of practice in education support the idea that teachers regularly assess their students to inform teaching practice. Some communities, however, differ regarding certain practices. For instance, some educator-affiliated communities would endorse the use of books that address racism or LGBTQIA+ issues as a way to honor all students' lives and experiences. Other communities oppose the use of books that address these topics. Some educational circles believe that the use of standardized curricula in schools constitutes equitable instruction because students are assured roughly the same level of instruction, but in other circles, a reliance on such curricula is considered inequitable because it may not meet all students' needs or be culturally congruent with their lives. And so there can be boundaries between communities of practice. If you are currently working as a teacher or teacher apprentice, you have probably encountered these boundaries, leaving you conflicted about what you are supposed to know and do. *Should I uphold scripted teaching even though it doesn't connect with students' lives?* Such boundaries, however, can offer rich opportunities for inquiry, discovery, and collaboration. You might ask: *How can I document my students' reactions to scripted teaching? How might I think about dismantling this practice? Who might I talk to or reach out to as I begin to engage in this process?*

In the landscape of practice model, "learning is not merely the acquisition of knowledge" (Wenger-Trayner & Wenger-Trayner, 2015, p. 19), but it is how we come to see ourselves in relation to the practices we engage in, people we speak with, the teaching frameworks we read about, and so forth. Finding oneself in a community requires engaging in the practices associated with this community, imagining ourselves as members of the community, and being able to align our practice to certain agreed-upon norms within the community. In some cases, teachers will find themselves at home in a well-aligned community, but in others, teachers will feel isolated, alienated, or even stuck when their community values don't align with their own, or when teaching practices they disagree with are mandated. For those who find themselves in the latter camp, it's important to remember you are not alone; whether it is on-site kinship or exploring other avenues for support via professional organizations and online communities, you can find your circle. To be an advocacy-focused teacher means *engaging* in the kinds of things they do, such as reading about inequalities at the school and societal levels, following advocacy-focused teachers on Instagram, or attending advocacy-focused professional development workshops. It means *imagining* yourself doing equity work in a particular type of school as a result of listening to, reading about, dialoguing with, and observing equity-oriented literacy teachers. It also means *aligning* your ways of thinking and doing with a larger emerging community of advocacy-focused educators.

For Laura, literacy teaching and advocacy are entwined. From her high expectations of her students' literacy potential, to the books she chooses, to the way she builds on students' knowledge traditions in her literacy lessons, there is no separation between pedagogical and advocacy practices for her. Her commitment to students and her competence as a literacy teacher is deeply connected to her understanding about equity and the race-based injustices of schooling and society that work against her students. Through this understanding and a love for *her* kids, she has positioned herself as their relentless advocate. A key part of becoming an advocacy-focused educator, then, is to connect issues of equity with literacy/language teaching practice, and be in the company of advocacy-focused teachers who enable us to imagine doing this work.

The problem is that advocacy-focused literacy teaching is not cemented in the "regime of competence" for educators. For instance, in university literacy methods classrooms and professional development sessions, critical discussions about equity are often left out of discussions about literacy pedagogy. Instead, discussions focus on methodologies of literacy teaching such as close reading, assessing writing, or vocabulary instruction. Explicit connections between elements of literacy teaching practice and issues of equity are rarely made. This means that many teachers have not been able to make explicit connections between pedagogical practice and equity/advocacy practice. Equally problematic is that, even if they have had these opportunities, more and more teachers are finding themselves working in climates that are actively hostile to making such explicit connections. In either case, it may be difficult to find model teachers who are practicing in advocacy-focused ways.

Filling the void in the current landscape of practice for teaching requires creating communities of practice that explicitly link issues of equity, including examinations of self, others, and the socio-political-cultural-historical contexts that shape learning and teaching, with issues of teaching, literacy, and language. We conceptualize this idea in Figure 1.1.

Creating these linkages expands the regime of competence for teachers to include advocacy work. To imagine, or perhaps reimagine, what this work looks like, we have filled this book with the voices and vignettes of teachers who are either doing this work or are trying to do it in their schools. Some of these teachers follow other teachers who are engaged in advocacy-focused literacy teaching via various social media platforms, while others pay close attention to students' social and emotional states and popular culture and their communication with caregivers and community members. These advocacy-focused educators notice, name, and correct inequities in their literacy classrooms and schools. They establish positive relationships with caregivers, make ongoing, explicit, and thoughtful connections between literacy teaching/learning and issues of equity, and draw from students' knowledge traditions to create culturally affirming classrooms.

We use the term "pathways" in the title of this book because we believe there are many ways to become advocacy-focused literacy teachers. This book represents one of many possible communities of practice that can put you on a path to engaging in, imagining, and aligning with others in this landscape of practice.

Figure 1.1. A Framework for Connecting Equity and Teaching

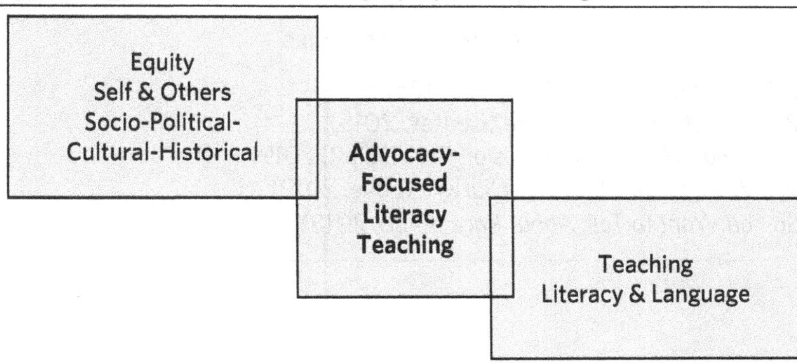

CONCLUSION

We began the chapter by introducing Ta-Nehisi Coates, a literary giant who recounted his resentment of schools in his book *Between the World and Me*. Why is it this way for millions of kids? We say it doesn't have to be. We literacy educators play a key part in creating safe, loving, culturally affirming literary worlds for students in our literacy classrooms, something akin to what Coates received in his own home. He was raised in a loving and literacy-rich home. His parents understood the wider sociopolitical history of racial disenfranchisement that impacts people of color. They immersed him in texts that reflected his experiences and heritage, used literacy to foster his intellectual curiosity, and most of all, they saw him as full of promise. Coates's questions about the world and his need for answers were centered in his home "curriculum." His questions *were* the curriculum. Being surrounded with books that reflected his heritage and people who were invested in supporting his intellectual growth fortified his cultural knowledge, sustained his intellectual curiosity, refined his critical abilities, and allowed him to identify as someone who uses language in powerful ways. Isn't that what we want for all kids?

We need to bring these same orientations and understandings to our literacy classrooms to see and nurture all students' fullest literacy capacities. No matter how many effective literacy teaching techniques we know, we will not be able to teach kids to read if we underestimate their abilities or blame their families or communities for their inability to meet grade-level literacy expectations. Despite all the research studies, all the testing, all the "scientifically based" literacy programs, and the seemingly endless debates about which literacy teaching method is best, there are still far too many students who do not realize their fullest literacy potential, and we educators *can* do something about it.

There are many pathways for becoming advocacy-focused literacy teachers. We chose to begin this work by examining ourselves and others through lenses of race and culture in the next chapter.

Recommended Books

- *Letter to My Daughter* (Angelou, 1987)
- *Between the World and Me* (Coates, 2015)
- *Teaching When the World Is on Fire* (Delpit, 2019)
- *We Want to Do More Than Survive* (Love, 2019)
- *So You Want to Talk About Race* (Oluo, 2018)

CHAPTER 2

Understanding Ourselves and Others

We do not learn from experience . . . we learn from reflecting on experience.

—John Dewey (1933)

Before any flight takes off, a flight attendant addresses passengers by saying: "In the event of a sudden loss of cabin pressure, an oxygen mask will drop from above. Secure your own mask before assisting others." Secure your own before assisting others . . . that sounds like a logical approach to many things, including understanding ourselves and our identities. Before we, as educators, can go into our classrooms to encourage our students to see themselves, love themselves, and honor who they are, we need to do the same. Unlike on an airplane, though, we often don't secure our own masks first—or, do the work to understand ourselves—at a moment in time when there is an emergency. We need to do the work of knowing ourselves and others as a foundation for advocacy-focused teaching. It is a lifelong commitment and it evolves and changes as we do.

In this chapter, we ask you to think about your race, culture, and intersectional identities. These are not easy tasks, and we use the word "developing" purposefully. Developing a truly critical awareness of ourselves and others takes time and reflection far beyond the "Pause and Reflect" prompts that we provide in these chapters. We hope you settle in and think about how you can secure your understanding as a way to best nurture your students' fullest literacy capacities.

DEVELOPING A CRITICAL AWARENESS OF RACE

Our campus sits on a demarcation line between the primarily white community of Lower Merion and the mostly Black community of Overbrook, a subsection of Philadelphia. Our geography is a constant reminder that de facto segregation continues to keep communities racially separate, with material consequences for residents' access to excellent schools and safe neighborhoods; Lower Merion is on the favored side. This is why race should matter to all future educators: It is relevant. We begin with these questions:

How racially literate are you? How does this matter to supporting students' literacy achievement?

While many of our undergraduate teaching candidates are white, about half of our graduate teacher candidates are people of color. Many of our white-affiliating teacher candidates and teachers have not had opportunities to interrogate the systemic advantages of whiteness, and relatively few can speak authentically about the talents, hopes, and dreams of students of color and their families. Nor have they been able to cultivate understandings about the cultural wealth and community networks that support youth of color (Yosso, 2005). When asked to describe themselves, most do not identify as white, but instead affiliate with the ethnic communities of their elders. *I'm Italian. I'm Irish. I'm half-Lithuanian and half-Polish.* Some use the archaic term *Caucasian* to describe themselves and other white-affiliating folks. Relatively few say they "do not see color." Lacking formal opportunities to study whiteness and how it has worked to their advantage, they sometimes speak and write in ways that have damaging consequences. Shoshanna testifies to this as a teacher educator in a primarily white teacher education program:

> As a Black female educator teaching at an affluent primarily white institution, there is not a day on campus that I am not reminded of my race and gender. While I want to promote an anti-racist, pro-feminist paradigm to the class discussions, I'm always aware I need to tow the line so as not to ruffle too many feathers. During the pandemic, this was particularly difficult. With all the civil unrest going on around the nation, I was stunned with some of the comments that my white students say as it related to students/people of color. On several occasions, I could feel myself wanting to scream, "Are you kidding me right now? Nobody deserves to be treated like that!" The struggle to get some students to understand the level of privilege they have is astounding at times. I sometimes ask myself: Is this really worth it?

Our undergraduate teacher candidates explore issues of race and racism in the first 2 years of our program while also apprenticing in schools with students of color, including emergent bilinguals. Many also attend schoolwide events that focus on issues of social justice and equity, sponsored by our school and other entities on campus. In our classrooms, we professors share our own testimonies of grappling with issues of race/racism, and how we will work on this indefinitely. By the time candidates enter the teacher candidacy program in their junior year, most have moved beyond *colorblindness,* a state of pretending not to notice color or acknowledge the existence of racism. Many can point out some overt examples of how systemic racism is manifested in schools. Most, however, do not yet know how they might work on the problem of racial injustice through their future teaching roles. The next step is acquiring a wide-eyed awareness of how whiteness is present in curricular choices, school assessment and teaching practices, educators' communication and relationships with caregivers, and other elements of schooling. When candidates are able to notice and name the ways racism operates through these elements, they will be positioned to actively challenge and work with others to dismantle racist practices.

While all educators are susceptible to the racist messaging that is omnipresent in U.S. society, studies have shown that white teachers are more likely to see Black children as less capable and in need of "being controlled" (Winfield, 1986) than teachers of color. Cultural conflicts between white teachers and students of color often explain students' academic difficulties and their misidentification with school (Au, 1980; Au & Jordan, 1981; Erickson, 1987). Underlying these conflicts are teachers' deficit assumptions about students' abilities and intentions. Deficit assumptions of students' academic abilities emerge as a result of being socialized into a culture of racism and white supremacy, a point we will return to later.

We are not saying that white teachers can't teach kids of color. Gloria Ladson Billings, a well-known researcher and author of the groundbreaking book *The Dreamkeepers: Successful Teachers of African American Children* (2009) pointed out that three of the eight highly successful teachers she studied were white. Like the other African American teachers Ladson-Billings studied, the white teachers in this group believed that all of their students could succeed and behaved in ways that nurtured their students' learning. What we are saying is that white educators, especially those who are disconnected from communities of color, may need to do more self-work to be in a place where they can see and nurture the literacy capacities of students of color. This means connecting with and learning about students' families, communities, experiences, and heritage. Kaitlin recalls how a more seasoned colleague guided her to learn from caregivers:

> As a 3rd-year teacher, I was finally starting to feel competent and confident in the procedures, teaching practices, curricula, etc., that I was so overwhelmed by during my first two years in the classroom. Teaching cross-culturally, I also felt like I had grown significantly in terms of establishing and maintaining reciprocal relationships with families. My knowledge of and appreciation for the community I was working in had also grown. As a kindergarten teacher, I was uniquely positioned to be able to spend time welcoming students' families at the start of the year as was required by the school. By Year 3, I thought I had my welcome meeting agenda down, and that it reflected the reciprocity that I was looking to foster. Then I spoke to a colleague who was also white, but seasoned and widely heralded for her phenomenal ability to engage students and families. I asked to compare our welcome agendas. I found that they were similar except for one gaping hole, a question that she opened with and one that I had left out entirely. Her meeting began with: "Tell me about [child's name]. What are your hopes and dreams for him/her this year and beyond?" Starting that year, I too opened with it. I cannot overstate the impact that this question had on every aspect of my approach to students and families.

While Kaitlin was fortunate to have a colleague who could steer her in the right direction to know her students' families, not all teachers have such assistance. Developing relationships with students, caregivers, and the community is integral to building racial literacy.

Teachers of color tend to see the capacities of students who share their racial affiliation, but they may still be operating according to absorbed racial biases as a consequence of living in a racist society. In his book *How to Be An Antiracist*, Ibram X. Kendi (2019) writes about his deeply held racial biases and how it took him decades to unpack these ideas to the point where he could grapple with them. In his book he agonizingly recalled denigrating Black youth in his high school graduation speech: *I kept shooting out unproven and disproven racist ideas about all the things wrong with Black youth—ironically, on the day when all the things right about Black youth were on display.* Similarly, April Baker-Bell (2020) observes that both educators of color and white educators perpetuate linguistic violence by insisting that Black students replace Black Language (BL) with white mainstream English (WME) in schools and in formal settings. Doing so communicates that students' language is inferior, and therefore students are inferior (Baker-Bell, 2020). The bottom line is that racial bias can exist within all of us and be absorbed in unconscious ways as a result of living in a society that transmits racialized messages through a variety of channels, including interpersonal communication, media, literacy, and work life.

Several identity frameworks describe how people across multiple racial/ethnic groups come to understand race and racism and act according to these understandings. Racial identity growth has been explained for those affiliating as African American (Vandiver et al., 2001), Asian/Pacific Islander (Kim, 2001), Latinx (Ferdman & Gallegos, 2001), biracial (Poston, 1990), and white (Helms, 1995). Racial identity growth typically begins with blindness to systemic racism, to growing levels of racial/ethnic awareness and understanding of race-based systems of advantage/disadvantage, toward the acquisition of positive racial identities. While these models provide lenses for viewing identity development and entry points for self-reflection, they are not meant to apply to all who identify with a particular racial/ethnic community, nor do they suggest that all people will experience racial identity growth in the same ways or in a linear fashion.

Since most educators of color live in near-constant awareness of race, the responsibility for understanding the way race works falls heavily on white teachers. White teacher candidates and teachers need to unpack their interactions with family, friends, films, television, social media, and other social portals that have shaped their ways of thinking about race, no matter how painful or embarrassing this process might be. If white teachers don't do this internal work, they cannot be open to the students they are serving. They may say or do things that will harm and traumatize students of color, and as a consequence, students will see school as a hostile place and will disconnect from it. School disengagement is one reason why so many students of color don't actually "drop out" of school—they are pushed out. Once pushed out, it is too late to recognize the beauty of students' language or their unique insights about texts. It is too late to offer them mind-expanding experiences that involve composing and interpreting texts in meaningful ways. The opportunity to be an uplifting presence for students in schools is forever gone.

A PATHWAY TO UNDERSTANDING

Using the metaphor of an archaeological dig, Yolanda Sealey-Ruiz (2021) invites educators to excavate our *racial literacy*—and particularly, how issues of race live deeply within us. Her model of *racial literacy development* includes six components: critical love, critical humility, critical reflection, historical literacy, archaeology of self, and interruption (p. 6). These components are visually arranged to form a pyramid, with the concept of critical love and the personal commitment to justice forming the limits of our own worldviews and ideologies. Then comes *critical reflection*, or the need to "think through the various layers of our identities and how privileged and marginalized status affect our work." *Historical literacy* involves developing "a rich and contextual awareness of the historical forces that shape the communities we work in but also the society we live in." *Archaeology of self* happens when we "begin a deep excavation and exploration of beliefs, biases, and ideas that shape how we engage in the work." Finally, *interruption* is at the top of the pyramid. It is manifested by our actions to "interrupt racism and inequality at personal and systemic levels." These components are intertwined and mutually dependent.

Sharing our archaeological digs with teacher candidates is an important step. First, we talk about how all of us have been shaped by American ideals of individualism and *meritocracy*—that achievement is dependent on one's own abilities, efforts, and skills. Many of our undergraduate students see their successes as a result of their own skills and efforts, and not in relation to the kinds of high-quality institutions and supportive social systems they have been afforded through their membership in racially or culturally dominant communities (Oakes & Lipton, 2002). Meritocratic views of themselves and the world prompt some teacher candidates to ask: *I studied hard; why can't they? My parents read to me; why can't theirs?*

Interrupting meritocratic notions requires coming to terms with whiteness and white privilege. White folks do not need to worry that the color of their skin will be held against them when applying for a car loan, filling out a job application, or renting an apartment. These are automatic, unearned advantages just for affiliating as white. The term *white privilege* is used to describe the collective advantage of whiteness in the United States and in many other parts of the world. We know it irritates and offends some white teacher candidates when they hear about white privilege, especially if they come from economically stressed families. Taking out student loans for thousands of dollars, driving a clunker car, wearing hand-me-downs, or being the first in your family to go to college are experiences that do not make you *feel* privileged. We get that. There are vast numbers of white people who have been locked in generational poverty for many reasons, including underfunded public education and jobs that have been shipped elsewhere. And while class issues may have made life difficult for millions of white folks, the one thing that they haven't had to deal with is the additional burden of racism. This point resonated with Althier when she dug into her life story and found the ways she had benefited directly from white advantage:

> At the age of 4, I attended a government-sponsored preschool program for poor and working-class families. We lived in a home bought by my grandfather, whose parents emigrated to the United States from Sicily when he was 4 years old. His dark complexion, his name (Rosario), and his Italian language marked him as a low-status immigrant. The other kids called him "WOP"—a racial slur used for Italian immigrants meaning "With Out Papers." His teacher changed his name to Charlie, a name his family embraced. It sounded white and American. They lived in "the Blocks," a housing project near the woolens mill where he worked after [completing] 6th grade. In time, Charlie proved to be a dependable worker, and was promoted to supervisor. His dream was to own a business. A private club for World War II soldiers stationed at nearby Camp Myles Standish was up for sale. Charlie did not have the funds to buy it, but he was able to secure a $5,000 loan from a local bookie. After the war ended, the club became a popular hangout for women attending the local college. As Charlie ran the business, he bought more town property, including houses that he rented, and educated his sons at Catholic schools. In the late 1960s, a fire nearly destroyed the club. With the help of his adult sons, he rebuilt and transformed it into a successful restaurant.

In writing a longer version of this story (Lazar, 2004), Althier marked instances where Charlie's whiteness worked to his advantage. She wondered about the likelihood that a person of color in the 1940s would have been promoted to a factory supervisor and or given a loan to buy a business. For her grandfather, Charlie, these opportunities translated to material and educational advantages for Charlie's descendants, including Althier's father John, who became a civil engineer and worked for the State of Massachusetts in 1960. In addition to obtaining secure employment, John was able to live in a property that Charlie owned. He was also able to pick up part-time work at a family business. Althier further recounts the advantages bestowed upon her in school in the early 1960s, such as a curriculum that reflected her experiences and teachers who saw her potential. So while she had to take out college loans, she was seen by her teachers as college material and had cultivated enough academic skills to be successful in college. Despite Charlie's denigrated social status, he did not encounter the types of structural roadblocks that were present for African Americans during his lifetime. Whiteness clearly worked in Charlie's favor, and it continues to work to his descendants' advantage. If you identify as white and do not believe you were advantaged by your whiteness, we suggest that you trace your ancestry through at least one elder who came of age in the first half of the 20th century and compare it to the likely experience of most people of color who grew up during the same time period.

Another legacy of white supremacy is *colorism,* the preference for lighter skin tones. Lighter skin has historically been equated with economic and social advancement. During the period of American enslavement, skin tone determined who toiled in the cotton fields and who worked in the Big House. Colorism is the reason why people all over the world lighten their skin with chemicals and why skin bleaching is an $8 billion industry. The only way to eliminate colorism, and acts of physical disfigurement that go along with it, is to dismantle white supremacy. We ask that you now take a moment to reflect on your own racial ancestry.

PAUSE AND REFLECT

1. Record the opportunities available to or denied to one of your elders, based on the history of inequitable policies and structures that were in place during that elder's lifetime.
2. In what ways have your current lifestyle and opportunities been shaped by this history?

STUMBLING AND GETTING BACK UP AGAIN

As we do the archaeological work of uncovering where our beliefs, biases, and privileges come from, we need to acknowledge that nobody is going to get it right 100% of the time. We, a group of scholar educators who study and teach about racial literacy development, continue to mess up, and in the aftermath, we continue to learn. Here's an example of Kaitlin getting it wrong, and her conversation with Shoshanna about the impact:

Kaitlin: I teach our department's "Hallmark" graduate course on language and culture. As a white educator tasked with teaching this foundational course that involves discussions of race and equity, I am highly cognizant of my role and I remain engaged in my own racial literacy development. Needless to say, I still get it wrong. After the summer of 2020, I inserted a prompt into our first Discussion Board on the topic of "Racism, Culture, and Social Equity Teaching." The prompt read, "For many, the year 2020 was the start of significant conversations about the pervasive nature of racism in this country." For 3 semesters, students responded to this prompt without question. Then in the Spring of 2022, a graduate student called me out. She reminded me that in fact, Black and Brown Americans like herself, of whom there are many in this country, have been living these conversations since Emmett Till in 1955. Not only did my prompt not speak to her lived experience, it discounted it. With that, her introduction to me, to our program, to our "Hallmark" course was marred by the blindness of a single sentence. I immediately responded with an apology and an acknowledgement that my wording was dismissive, which I shared both individually with the student and then with the whole class.

Shoshanna: 2020 became the year we could no longer ignore the pervasive nature of racism. People of color have been talking about racism for years, but it was often difficult to get hard evidence to prove that it existed on so many levels. Without such evidence, many white people did not recognize the pervasiveness of racism. But now with people recording everything on cell phones, you can't say it doesn't exist. So maybe it seems like the start or a start, but people of color have struggled and protested for decades. You know, I also commend the student for even feeling comfortable enough to address this issue with you because that exchange could have gone very differently. Your response to her was acknowledging "Hey, you're absolutely right," which in and of itself is powerful. Allowing yourself to be vulnerable with the student and students to say, "You know what, I missed the mark on this . . ." is important. But also we have to understand that the student had to decide . . . "Do I start my semester by calling out this professor with the potential for blowback?" Because now that she's said this, she has to face the fact that she may be seen as the "problem" student, and she has to think about how her classmates are going to feel about her now because maybe they'll think she's "that person" or "that girl." It really does weigh on students of color. Our students struggle and it's exhausting, especially in certain spaces, like our campus, because it's constant.

The danger of a single prompt. We don't always get it right, but that doesn't mean we shouldn't try to. The role of educators is to cultivate, to encourage, to empower, to listen, to teach, to model . . . to support students in all the ways that don't contribute to the intellectual exhaustion of students of color. When screw-ups happen, we recognize, we reflect, we learn, and then we do better. Racial literacy development doesn't have a culmination point; there is no finale or summit because it's both a process and an evolution. We understand that you may be just starting to think about your ethical commitment to caring for students and the ways in which you and others have been privileged and subordinated by a number of social positions and identities. You may be just starting to recognize how historical and contemporary forces have shaped opportunities for minoritized students.

Racial literacy development is a forever journey, and it takes much more than reading this book or other books to support your growth. It's important for us to recognize that reality. We need to learn shoulder to shoulder with those who are already doing this work. Just as social media galvanized millions around the Black Lives Matter (BLM) movement, digital networks are spreading the word about what equity-oriented educators are thinking and how they are helping their students grapple with issues of race (Price-Dennis & Sealey-Ruiz, 2021). As you read this book, consider following and contributing to one or several Twitter groups (check out #Educate2Liberate; #TeachTruth; #RecognizingOurPower; #PaveTheWay; #d100inspires) so you can be part of a growing network of educators who are committed to racial literacy and empowering students to realize their fullest literacy potential. Let us pause now and consider what we are bringing to this work.

Pause and Reflect

1. Think about your levels of connection/disconnection from your students' communities. What kind of ethical commitment do you have to your students or future students?
2. How do you think your relationship to students' communities will shape your views of students and your teaching?
3. How might you learn more about the students and communities you are supposed to serve?

DEVELOPING A CRITICAL AWARENESS OF CULTURE

In addition to working on racial literacy, there is a need to develop other forms of sociocultural competence. As educators, we often talk to teacher candidates about culture, cultural identities, and related complexities and when we do, inevitably we see the same pattern. Here Kaitlin explains:

> When I have conversations about culture with teacher candidates, undergraduates in particular, I find that there is this instinct to boil culture down to

> three things: music, holidays, and food. Hard as I may try, it feels like there is this hang-up related to some cultural trifecta. It takes an immense amount of thought and unpacking to undo this pattern. It's like a default setting.

In the literacy classroom, a superficial focus on heroes, holidays, and cultural tours of the world means that deeper cultural issues related to beliefs, practices, values, and ways of looking at the world are not explored. Reading books, writing narratives and essays, designing podcasts, interpreting social media—all of these literacies involve unpacking the deeper dimensions of culture. This is why investigating culture needs to be part of working the boundary between equity, literacy, and language.

Culture is far from a default setting. It is a dynamic and evolving set of shared values, beliefs, understandings, and practices that allow members of social groups to communicate and work together (Hudelson, 2004). Educators and students can operate from very different values, beliefs, understandings, and practices. Understanding your own and others' beliefs and practices around language and literacy is an important place to start, and we offer guidance for this in Chapter 5. Communicating successfully with students and their families, and employing culturally sustaining approaches in the classroom, requires that we educators be invested in understanding culture—our own and our students'. Our teaching success depends on it.

Let's consider how people identify themselves culturally. All of us identify as members of different groups who share particular values, beliefs, and practices. Some groups hold more power, or access to opportunities, than other groups in a given society. In America, power has traditionally been associated with being white, affluent, male, Christian, English-speaking, heterosexual, a U.S. citizen, able-bodied, and other *culturally dominant* identity positions.

Some of us affiliate with groups whose rights and freedoms have been historically denied or threatened and therefore we identify ourselves on the basis of being a member of a *minoritized* group. *I'm Black. I'm Jewish. I'm Gay.* The term *minoritized* calls attention to the power divisions among groups of people and the continuing struggle to overcome injustices. *BIPOC,* a popular term that refers to Black, Indigenous and people of color, is an inclusive way to refer to some minoritized groups. *LGBTQIA+* (lesbian, gay, bisexual, transgender, queer/questioning, intersex, agender/asexual, and more) is another inclusive way to refer to minoritized groups on the basis of sexual identification. We can also look at marginalization from the perspectives of language, religion, and citizenship. Immigrants, speakers of languages other than English, Muslims, and undocumented individuals are minoritized, as are people with ability differences.

We find that many folks still use the word *minority* when referring to members of minoritized communities, but this term reflects a white-dominant orientation: One is a "minority" *relative to white people.* In many communities, the so-called minority groups constitute the majority. If we look at the demographics nationally, people of color will constitute the majority of U.S. citizens by 2045.

Cultural affiliation gets more complicated because it shifts depending on what's happening politically, socially, and economically. There are times when it makes sense for groups that are linked by common ancestry or geographical origin to join together in solidarity for sociopolitical reasons. In the months following the outbreak of the COVID-19 pandemic, some on the political right blamed the Chinese government and China's scientific community for intentionally spreading the virus. The fallout in the United States was that people who affiliate as Asian American and Pacific Islander (AAPI) were threatened, brutally beaten, and even murdered. Even though members of this coalition can trace their ancestry to over 30 different countries and ethnic groups in East Asia, Southwest Asia, and the Indian subcontinent, the common threat imposed upon them resulted in many asserting a strong AAPI identity. One of our colleagues, Grace Lee (pseudonym), strongly affiliated as Taiwanese American prior to the pandemic, but has since gravitated toward identifying with a broader coalition of Asian Americans—whose lifestyles are now determined by a looming threat of violence imposed by xenophobic, anti-immigrant, white supremacist, and ultra-nationalist groups. Grace discussed the choices she now has to make and how she copes with the latest regime of terror against members of AAPI communities:

> I'm not comfortable walking in the city by myself. It is weird because I went to undergraduate and graduate school in two different East Coast cities. I'm now in a space where I meet that demographic, the older Asian female. So now I don't go to cities alone. I always make sure someone is with me. I have to pay attention to where I park the car and what restaurants I go to. So how does that make me feel? Initially, I was angry. Why should I be afraid? I've lived here most of my life. I've contributed to society in many ways. I do whatever it is that makes me a good citizen. Now I have to deal with these assumptions, just based on how I look. Everyone deals with this awareness differently. Some people joined protest rallies. I don't do that because I don't think it works. Activism for me works more through being a leader in my organization. Through different leadership roles, you are showing that the voice that you represent matters. It also helped that I'm part of some Asian Pacific support groups. One in particular is where I find a lot of support. I'm learning a lot from that group. I also use testimonials to interrogate where I am culturally. I ask myself what it means to be Chinese, a woman, and an American. I think it will be a continuous journey.

Affiliating as AAPI offers Grace and others a line of defense against the violence targeting this community. Identifying with the larger coalition group provides members with strength in numbers to challenge several other pertinent issues, such as the erasure and misrepresentation of their history and experiences within the school curriculum, the "model minority" myth, and the "perpetual foreigner" stereotype (Hsieh & Kim, 2020).

Similarly, many people who trace their ancestry to different countries in Latin America may affiliate as *Latinx* or *Latino/Latina*. Though we will use Latinx here, we acknowledge that this gender-neutral term, which is meant to be inclusive, has been the subject of recent pushback from Latino civil right organizations that feel it misrepresents how some Latinos prefer to define themselves. Members of this group may identify as *Brown* to describe their minoritized status in the United States. Many members affiliate as Latinx to battle specific political campaigns, such as anti-immigration laws. When Donald Trump labeled migrants from Mexico as rapists, murderers, and drug traffickers, many in the Latinx community banded together to denounce him. Like the AAPI coalition, the Latinx diaspora is highly complex. Many of those who affiliate as Cuban American and who experienced firsthand the Communist overthrow of Cuba in the 1960s identify as Republican, while some other Latinx groups who seek to change discriminatory and racist laws affiliate as Democrats.

Affiliating as *Black* also has a complex sociopolitical history. During the Civil Rights Movement, identifying as Black stood for challenging generational racism, instilling racial pride, and asserting self-determination. As we indicated earlier, the fight for racial equality continues today through the BLM movement. In Philadelphia, Black activism is alive and well, with community groups protesting the closure of neighborhood schools, acts of racial discrimination, and police brutality. When two Black men were arrested at a downtown Starbucks merely because they sat down for a meeting and asked to use the restroom without having purchased anything, activists took to the streets in protest. While Black identity is politically rooted, groups that affiliate as Black have distinct histories, experiences, and languages. Multigenerational descendants of free and enslaved Africans often share very different cultural orientations from those who recently immigrated from Africa and the West Indies.

Even if individuals within a specific geographic/ancestry group share certain orientations and experiences, each individual within these groups is uniquely positioned and shaped by their socioeconomic status, gender identity, religion, citizenship status, language, sexual orientation, and other social/identity positions. In other words, a racial, ethnic, or minoritized group is not a monolith. To assume that all who affiliate with a certain group think or act in certain ways is flawed thinking. Cultural identity is further complicated by the reality that many of us come from multiracial backgrounds and choose to identify as biracial or mixed race. All of this is to say that cultural identification is both political and deeply personal.

DEVELOPING A CRITICAL AWARENESS OF INTERSECTIONALITY

Each of us is a composite of many identities related to race, ethnicity, gender, religion, language competence, sexual identity, citizenship status, physical ability, and we could go on. Each of these identity markers is assigned a particular power status, depending on the values that a given society attaches to it. Legal scholar Kimberlé Crenshaw (1989) invented the term *intersectionality* to describe how multiple forms of disadvantage can compound to create obstacles for people who affiliate with oppressed identity groups. Intersectionality is important because it helps us consider how race conflates with other identities in ways that shape people's lives and opportunities.

Bettina Love (2019) examines the hard questions of intersectionality when she refers to Morris' research on "age compression," as a state "in which Black girls are seen as Black women, with all the stereotypes that go along with Black womanhood (e.g., hypersexual, loud, rude, and aggressive)" (p. 5). Love asks educators to consider how various cross-sections of identity impact the lives and experiences of students:

> What does this school reality mean for Black girls who are part of the LGBTQ community, Black girls who are Muslim, Black girls who are immigrants, Black girls who are disabled, and Black girls who are incarcerated or formerly incarcerated. What does this school reality mean for a Latinx girl who is queer, undocumented, and disabled? How do Black girls who are a combination of these identities deal with the complexities and the realities of discrimination, harassment, and violence?

Recognizing how classrooms and schools are unresponsive to Black girls' identities and academic needs is one reason why Black women literacy scholars have come together to create the Black Girls' Literacies Collective Statement (NCTE, 2018), to "call out and work against educational harm toward Black women and girls, while simultaneously promoting their social and academic success" (p. 173).

Kaitlin asks similar questions about the intersection of race and gender when it comes to zero tolerance policies, suspensions, and expulsions aimed at very young Black boys. Consider her conversations with Black mothers navigating urban childcare systems using subsidies. For many moms, suspension and expulsion were top of mind, despite their pre-K age children having been alive for just over a thousand days. Jule, a single mother of two working as a hairstylist, whose 4-year-old son had been asked to leave multiple settings, shared her family's struggles:

> I just found a good school, but I've been told he has real behavior issues by other places. I think it's a good pre-K. I think his teacher is really good, but I'm worried they're just not . . . I don't think they're too good at handling how many kids there are and how he is. . . . His teacher already said he would do better at a smaller place. I'm worried they aren't happy with him and he might get suspended. I don't want that to happen . . . again. I think these schools need help so they can learn how to deal with [kids] and if the parent really wants them to stay at the school they'll be able to stay.

The instances of caregivers being informed that their small children "had needs that could not be met," "would do much better in a different setting," or "were no longer welcome" suggest that racial and gender profiling starts very early for Black and Brown boys. Kaitlin's experiences are consistent with the research that describes Black boys' disproportionate school suspensions and expulsions as early as preschool (Gilliam et al., 2016; Wright & Counsell, 2018). Age compression is a factor in perceptions of Black boys. Educators tend to view these youngsters as older than they are, resulting in their being subjected to more stringent and punitive discipline practices (Wright & Counsell, 2018). In literacy classrooms, curricula and teaching often limit Black boys' ability to connect with their ancestral lineage of reading for meaningful and relevant purposes or engage in collaborative reading experiences with peers (Tatum, 2009). Research also shows that schools do not tend to promote Black boys' identification as writers and future authors (Haddix, 2009). Such findings have paved the way for promising literacy teaching practices to find ways to affirm Black boys' identities and nurture their school literacy engagements (Everett & Moten, 2022; Husband & Kang, 2020; Tatum, 2014).

These trends illustrate how intersectionality can be an important conceptual lens for looking at how schools shape the particular experiences of those who share subjugated identities. We need to be mindful about how the confluence of gender, race, sexuality, and other identities position people in marginalized or advantaged ways. Understanding how we see students through our own multiple intersectional identities is an important attribute of advocacy-focused teachers.

Pause and Reflect

1. How have you witnessed the ways subordinated groups have coalesced around a cause?
2. In what ways are you privileged? In what ways are you subordinated?
3. How might your intersectional identities shape the way you see students?

CONCLUSION

We can't interrupt racism unless we see ourselves as responsible for perpetuating racist structures. We can't understand the historical forces that shape communities unless we take a long look at how we've been privileged and/or marginalized on the basis of our social positions, and how these positions have been historically shaped. Those of us who have not interrogated our own histories of privilege and subordination or who deny the existence of systemic racism and other "isms" are disconnected from the lived realities of people who are routinely marginalized. Exploring these issues, however, will deepen and enrich the ways you see children, communities, and literacy teaching. One place to start is to look further at the positions taken by those we are citing in this book. We also recommend that you become familiar with inclusive and culturally affirming language. Check out this website for a list of inclusive terms: https://multicultural.utah.gov/poweroflanguage/.

Keep securing, keep exploring. You come to this profession as you are, with unique identities and experiences, and with the capacity to continue to learn and grow. We recognize the strengths and challenges in our students and scaffold accordingly and we invite you to do the same with yourself. We invite you to think about where you are on your journey to developing critical awareness of race, culture, and intersectionalities and to grow from that place, wherever it may be. It won't happen overnight; progress may be painful and it may be slow, but it's your commitment to the process that will be most beneficial, not just for you, but for all of those who sit beside you on your journey—your students, their families, your colleagues, the school community. It is only when your emergency mask is secure that you can assist others.

Recommended Books

- *Inventing Latinos: A New Story of American Racism* (Gómez, 2020)
- *Minor Feelings: An Asian American Reckoning* (Hong, 2020)
- *Hood Feminism: Notes from the Women that a Movement Forgot* (Kendall, 2020)
- *How to Be an Antiracist* (Kendi, 2019)
- *The Dreamkeepers: Successful Teachers of African American Children* (Ladson-Billings, 2009)
- *The Making of Asian America* (Lee, 2016)

CHAPTER 3

Inequities in Schools and Classrooms

> **The child who is not embraced by the village will burn it down to feel its warmth.**
>
> **—African Proverb (Mobe, n.d.)**

One pathway for becoming advocacy-oriented teachers involves taking a close look at societal inequities that impact school literacy learning. School literacy learning opportunities are inequitably distributed in the United States (Baker-Bell, 2020; Milner, 2019; Picower, 2021). In economically distressed communities that serve high percentages of students of color, the cumulative effects of racial segregation, concentrated poverty, and educational funding disparities converge to reduce students' access to vital schooling resources. These resources include experienced teachers, fully functioning libraries, teaching support personnel, and learning resources (Carter & Welner, 2013). In addition, Euro-focused curricula and one-size-fits-all approaches to teaching and assessment prevent too many students from succeeding according to school expectations.

In this chapter, we take up just some of the major issues plaguing schools in Philadelphia and beyond, including why minoritized students are so frequently pushed out of schools, how schools have become "culturally alienating" places for students; why the disjuncture between home literacies and standardized English dismisses students' knowledge traditions; and how minoritized students continue to be undermined by standardized curricula, widespread testing, and underfunded school systems. Next, we take a look at the literacy classroom, examining how common practices, including teaching routines and structures, further disenfranchise minoritized students by repressing opportunities for creative and complex thinking and sending students the message that they are less capable than they truly are. Finally, we address the damage that deficit descriptions and approaches inflict on BIPOC students and communities.

Why do we bring attention to these issues? Calling out the obstacles that prevent students from realizing their full literacy potential is necessary because many of these barriers have become so normalized in schools that we tend not to notice them. And when we don't notice and name them, we cannot do anything to challenge them. So here we go.

PUSHING KIDS OUT OF SCHOOL

It has only been in recent years that educators have started to seriously challenge the narrative that one of the most persistent problems in our schools is that students of color frequently drop out of school—high school in particular. To suggest that students drop out assumes that they leave willingly. The term "drop out" obscures the complicated nature of students' departure from school. It also places the blame of school departure squarely on the shoulders of students when the reality is that students of color are regularly "pushed out," or in some cases, "pulled out" of school.

Theories and theoretical models that speak to students being pushed out address how school structures interact with students' dispositions and behaviors to force departures. When students don't feel welcome, connected, and valued in our classrooms, they are likely to retreat from the academic process. This feeling often leads to externalizing behaviors and/or displays of academic apathy. Both result in students being punished, most often through highly punitive and liberally applied suspension and expulsion practices.

The suspension and expulsion rates for BIPOC students are alarming, and they begin to impact children's academic progress as early as preschool. Make no mistake about it, disproportionate suspension and expulsion rates demonstrate that racial inequities are alive and well in our school system with Black and Latinx students being punished early and often. Consider that Black preschoolers, who make up just 19% of preschoolers, represent 47% of those suspended at this grade level (Gilliam et al., 2016), and that simply having higher percentages of Latinx children in an early childhood classroom is a strong predictor of higher suspension rates (Gilliam & Shahar, 2006). And the situation remains dire for these students as they age. Black students are between 2.19 and 3.78 times as likely as their white peers to be referred by teachers to the office for problem behavior in elementary school and middle school respectively (Bottiani et al., 2017; Kaufman et al., 2010; Skiba et al., 2002). Black and Latinx students are also more likely to receive harsher punishments (out-of-school suspensions and expulsions) for the same or similar behaviors when compared to their white peers. Punitive and exclusionary practices, which are in no way developmentally appropriate for children, lead to disruptions in academic progress. When young children of color are excluded from classrooms due to suspensions and/or expulsions, they miss instructional time, which can adversely impact their school readiness. Over time, the challenges minoritized students face begin to compound, resulting in systemic inequalities that fuel long-term health, wellness, and economic disparities (American Psychological Association [APA], Presidential Task Force on Educational Disparities, 2012; Balfanz et al., 2014; Shollenberger, 2015).

Academic disinterest is another major issue that contributes to push out. As has been well documented, students from economically stressed backgrounds and students of color are less likely to be identified as gifted and talented and they are disproportionately referred for special education services (Grissom & Redding, 2016). When programming for students completely dismisses their potential and/or misidentifies their strengths, interests, and needs, it's unreasonable for teachers, or anyone, to expect students to remain highly engaged in their academic progress. If schools refuse to recognize and appreciate qualities like brilliance and individuality in students of color, how can we turn around and blame these students for losing interest?

Pullout factors like family financial needs, teen parenthood, immigration issues, domestic abuse, and violence in communities are equally relevant, but less frequently cited reasons for school departure. As students from minoritized communities get older, many find themselves faced with "life stuff," or things that start to increasingly require their time and attention. Students with other commitments often experience difficulty fully participating in a largely one-size-fits-all education model. Rather than accommodate their realities, we have a system that forces students to weigh their options. When the cost–benefit analysis is conducted, many of our students experiencing "life stuff" find themselves pulled out of school. Shoshanna recently sat down with a local elementary and middle school art teacher, Amari Williams (pseudonym), to hear more about the factors that he sees as contributing to students leaving school.

> Black and Brown kids are constantly overlooked, misjudged, and counted out. Who really cares when they go absent for weeks at a time? Come to school hungry or disheveled? Can't read on grade level or struggle with rudimentary instructions from their teachers? I've known of kids who have left for all sorts of reasons. Mostly because they are taking on adult responsibilities like caring for younger siblings or ailing grandparents. And then there are the ones that are drawn to the streets following older siblings or kids in the neighborhood. Dropping out of school is not a taboo thing like it was when we went to school. The kids I used to work with were adjudicated youth. They had gotten in so much trouble in school, transferred all around and then finally sent to "group homes" as a last resort. By the time they arrived, they had long given up. They didn't see value in themselves or the educational system. The streets seem to embrace them in ways that the educational system did not. How can you blame them? The messages they receive daily suggest that they are not worthy of our time. Some teachers have very little patience for them and are quick to send them to the principal's office. One of my kids spent more time there than in my class.

Given this bleak picture, why show up? On top of the likelihood that students of color will be pushed or pulled out of schools, we also know that schools are culturally alienating places for BIPOC students. They often experience cultural and social alienation as soon as they enter the public education system (Christians, 2014; Nieto, 2000). Yet we still expect them to show up. Not only that, we tell students who do not feel seen, heard, or even welcome in our hallways and classrooms that they need to be actively engaged in acquiring school-valued literacies. Who wants to sign up for that?

While there is no quick fix to address alienation in all its forms, there is a plethora of research on how cultural and social alienation impacts BIPOC students' achievement and mental health. In 1992, Mau offered one of the first comprehensive perspectives on why students of color feel alienation in schools. This perspective posits that there are four overlapping dimensions that contribute, including: (1) powerlessness (e.g., disproportionately higher rates of suspension and expulsion for Black and Latinx students); (2) meaninglessness (e.g., curricula that erases, discounts, or makes invisible the histories and identities of those who identify as Black, Latinx, American Indian/Alaska Native, and Asian American/Pacific Islander); (3) normlessness (e.g., the perpetuation of whiteness as the normative school culture and the punishment of forms of expression that vary from it, like students demonstrating support for Black Lives Matter); and (4) social estrangement (e.g., emotional and/or physical disconnection from the school environment due to deficient or inappropriate programming that deters participation in activities, clubs, social events, etc.).

With concern for students' mental health needs at the forefront of many educators' minds, it's important to consider that when our students feel alienated, disconnected, withdrawn, disengaged, and discriminated against in our schools and classrooms, they are more likely to develop depressive symptoms (Seaton, 2009). The traumas of the past few years—disparate rates of people from minoritized communities becoming seriously ill or dying from COVID-19; job loss and financial insecurities; remote learning and social isolation; the murders of George Floyd, Tyre Nichols, and so many other Black men and women; mass shootings; violence that targets Black, AAPI, and LGBTQIA+ communities—have made the mental health needs of BIPOC students nothing short of pressing. Now, perhaps more than ever, it is critical that educators interrogate the factors that underlie cultural and social alienation in schools so as to not further isolate and harm our students. Let's pause here to consider the issues.

Pause and Reflect

1. Think back about your experiences as a student, intern teacher, or teacher. Think about the students who seemed disconnected with school, frequently absent, or routinely sent to the principal's office. Which of the factors discussed so far could account for their disengagement with school?

2. Look up the high school graduation rates in your home or work community before and after the pandemic. What school-wide efforts are educators making (or not making) to keep students engaged, valued, and feeling safe in the schools you know best?

LIMITATIONS OF LITERACY CURRICULA AND ASSESSMENT

Many teachers are expected to adhere to scripted curricula and meet testing mandates, especially those in economically stressed school districts. In literacy classrooms, curriculum mandates are increasingly predicated on a "science of reading" (SoR) construct that emphasizes basic reading processes and is rooted in experimental psychology (Hoffman et al., 2020). As expressed in schools, SoR often focuses narrowly on reading proficiency as measured by tests. This *simple view of reading* "holds that decoding proficiency and language proficiency (typically operationalized as listening comprehension) fully account for reading comprehension proficiency" (Aukerman & Chambers Schuldt, 2021, p. 86). We support literacy instruction based on rigorous research, but we take issue with research findings that are not based on culturally and linguistically diverse student populations, or ones that are grounded in narrow views of reading and assessment. We cannot afford to waste students' time on instructional approaches that do not lift all students.

There is no doubt that decoding and comprehension are essential parts of a scientifically based reading program. Explicit exposure to the English graphophonic system and teaching students to be fluent, automatic decoders of words frees up the mind to focus on understanding texts. This is irrefutable. The problem is that reading programs that are solely or primarily based on these two areas will not necessarily produce literate people who love to read; who can read texts critically; who can select and compose texts for their own goals and purposes; and who can see themselves as readers, writers, and thinkers (Aukerman & Chambers Schuldt, 2021, p. 85). An oversimplified view of reading means that educators may see students, and students may see themselves as lacking if they underperform on tests. This is why many educators are calling for more expansive SoR instructional frameworks that acknowledge students' linguistic, cultural, and individual variations and capacities, as well as their literacy dispositions and engagements across contexts.

Literacy researcher Nell Duke and her colleagues argue for a multifaceted view of a science of reading comprehension that includes teaching print and phonological awareness, phonics, morphology, word recognition, fluency, bridging (skills that bridge word reading and comprehension), vocabulary, comprehension strategies, text structures and features, and writing in response to reading (Duke et al., 2021). Further, their layered model holds that effective reading instruction must also consider students' motivation for reading, and that teaching be assessment-based, differentiated based on students' needs, culturally sustaining, equitable, and designed to honor students' identities and build relationships.

Unfortunately, many schools have not caught up with a more expansive view of SoR. In some of the classrooms we know, teachers are expected to use prepackaged programs that drill students on letter names and sounds. As we stated, explicit instruction in phonics is necessary, but teachers are being asked to teach all students the same letter or orthographic pattern at the same time. Such a practice violates a basic principle of learning. Learning happens when it is targeted to students' diverse zones of development (Vygotsky, 1978). Students bring vastly different experiences with literacy to the classroom. Some students already know the letter or orthographic pattern being presented, and should be learning something else. Other students may need more fundamental instruction, such as rhyming or onset-rimes. The decision to adopt one-size-fits-all literacy programs will translate to inequitable classroom practice if teachers are not expected to or shown how to differentiate instruction. We also know that very little writing happens in some literacy classrooms even though writing improves reading (Graham et al., 2018). If students are not writing in response to literature and writing for different purposes and to different audiences, they are being held back. Limiting writing in the literacy classroom is not only unscientific; it is inequitable.

Another inequity is the prioritization of standardized English in the curriculum, which presents a significant challenge for students for whom standardized English is not the norm. Access to this idealized norm is a "must have" for success in the system, from entry to exit. The reality is that it has become an expectation, and there is simply no space in many classrooms for deviation or variation. High-stakes standardized literacy tests based on mastery of academic English have had detrimental effects on students of color (Rosales & Walker, 2021; Souto-Manning, 2021), including multilingual learners (García & Kleifgen, 2018). For students whose lived experiences include the many other literacies and knowledge traditions that are vibrant within and across communities of color, adjusting to this expectation can be jarring. There is little, if any, acknowledgement that the literacies valued in their homes and communities even exist. Their literacy practices and ways of knowing are frequently not reflected in curricula, pedagogy, and assessment. And, unfortunately, too many teachers fail to recognize, let alone tap into, welcome, or celebrate, the many benefits of opening their classrooms to non-dominant literacies and knowledge traditions. We will circle back to this issue in Chapter 4.

The norming of standardized English gets reinforced through the use of standardized curricula and high-stakes testing, and exacerbates the challenges that many schools and districts face. Standardized curricula and testing has dominated Philadelphia classrooms for several years as a result of a series of federal initiatives that began with No Child Left Behind (NCLB) and that continue today with Common Core State Standards (CCSS). The residual influences of these initiatives leave many novice teachers scrambling to find spaces to individualize instruction and welcome students' knowledge traditions while also adhering to curriculum and testing mandates. We have regularly worked in schools and have seen how literacy instruction has become fused with test preparation. Althier found this to be true in a way that violated every notion that she had about teaching students to write:

> Literacy instruction, and in particular writing instruction, is designed around PSSA (Pennsylvania System of School Assessment) test questions. Students must read a passage in order to answer a prompt. Students are expected to restate the prompt, generate an opinion, list evidence from the passage to support their opinion, and restate their opinion. They are not taught authentic purposes for writing or that their writing would be read by an audience other than the teacher. Students are not shown how to select their own topics for writing, nor are they shown mentor texts from talented authors including those who look like them. They are not shown how their teacher approaches the writing process, nor are they shown how to revise or edit their writing. It was as if 30 years of writing process pedagogy had disappeared in the wake of NCLB.

The passing of NCLB in 2002 made the link between standardized curricula, high-stakes testing, and school funding inextricable. In an attempt to close what was then determined to be an "achievement gap" separating students along disparate racial/ethnic and socioeconomic lines, the federal government increased its role in public education. The bill's stated intention was to increase funding for poor school districts and increase the academic achievement of minoritized students, with high-stakes tests being used to measure their academic progress. Standardized curricula were adopted by these school districts, narrowing the curriculum to those subjects that were tested, primarily math and literacy. Teachers were expected to stick closely to mandated curriculum units, and were often expected to follow scripted lessons, which reduced opportunities for differentiated and culturally centered instruction. Kaitlin shares what it was like to teach in the immediate aftermath of NCLB's passage.

> I remember being astounded by the expectations for my ELA (English Language Arts) and math blocks when I moved up from pre-K to kindergarten just a few years after NCLB was adopted. My literacy block consisted of three "complimentary" scripted curricula and lasted an uninterrupted 120 minutes. My math block was 90 minutes long, but we only had two scripted curricula and my kids got a 20-minute lunch break in between them. After math, we had a 45-minute

> writing block. The party line answer on when I could teach social studies and science was that I could rotate between them in the afternoons if all ELA and math content had been covered. If all went well, kids could go to centers at the end of the day. These kids were 5 and 6 years old. On a good day, they could maybe sit for 10 minutes. I was so confused. It was understood that no one in my school building actually agreed with these expectations. In fact, we largely defied them as a school community without consequence. In reality, my class's schedule looked much different than it was "supposed to." I will also never forget the day that a huge stack of Scantron sheets were left on my desk by an unnamed source. On top, there was a typed note with instructions to have my students practice filling them out as part of their preparation for 1st grade. My grade group and I were absolutely horrified.

When districts and schools didn't make adequate yearly progress (AYP) based on testing, they did not receive desperately needed funding. Many schools were reconstituted; some states lowered their standards in an attempt to alleviate pressure, and the "gap" continued to grow.

While significant portions of NCLB have been walked back in the last decade through the passing of Every Student Succeeds Act (ESSA) in 2015 and the adoption of Common Core State Standards, its remnants continue to adversely impact students of color. Standardized curricula and high-stakes testing remain hallmarks of our public education system. Poor districts and schools remain underfunded. The "achievement gap" is now largely recognized to be an "opportunity gap," which reframes the problem as having to do with input (inequitable distribution of resources) rather than output (inequitable distribution of results) (Milner, 2017). But, the underlying issues remain. To understand the hold that they have on our schools, and students, look no farther than the federal government announcing that after a year "off" in 2020, state standardized tests would return in 2021 after over a year of unprecedented school disruption due to the ongoing global pandemic. Other fixtures, like the overrepresentation of students of color in high-incidence disability categories, and remedial programs like Response to Intervention, have failed to improve Black students' literacy achievement (Cramer, 2015; Willis, 2019). Let's pause to think about these issues.

PAUSE AND REFLECT

1. Consider the tasks that are expected of students when they take a standardized test (answering questions in a specified time period, reading short passages about unfamiliar subjects, filling in bubbles, responding to writing prompts, etc.). How might students whose literacies and languages differ from those valued in school react to these tasks?

2. In the schools that you intern or work in, what standardized tests are used and when do students take them? How much time is spent on test preparation? How do students respond to these tests?

LITERACY TEACHING ROUTINES AND STRUCTURES

Let's turn now to the literacy classroom as there too we see barriers that have become so normalized in schools we tend to forget that in reality they are preventing students from realizing their full literacy potential. There are many literacy teaching routines and structures that undermine students' literacy learning, including elements that we may not think are problematic, but are. They are problematic because they either disengage or frustrate students, squelch complex thinking, fail to move students forward in their growth, and/or communicate to students that they are less capable than they really are. In this section, we address the use of permanent ability grouping, using book levels to describe students, the overuse of low-level questioning, and the validation of teacher-approved communal responses to comprehension questions.

A popular structure for teaching reading is the guided reading group. These are small, teacher-led ability-based groups where students read and discuss books and learn various strategies and skills associated with proficient reading. The teacher generally introduces a leveled text to students by focusing on the content (e.g., *This book will teach us how animals take care of their babies; we are going to read to find out what they do*). The teacher may invite students to study the cover and title, think about what they already know about the subject, make predictions about what might happen, or invite students to do a picture walk to preview difficult vocabulary or point out an orthographic pattern that students will encounter while reading. Often, the teacher will introduce or model a word recognition or comprehension strategy that good readers use when they read independently (e.g., *Good readers often ask questions while they read*). The teacher then invites all students to "whisper read" or read silently while moving around the teaching table to monitor each child's reading and text understanding. After reading, the teacher often engages students in a discussion about the book, asking students to defend their responses by citing evidence from the text. Students may also discuss how they used a strategy to recognize words or read more proficiently.

On the surface, there is nothing objectionable about the practices associated with guided reading. This structure can become problematic, however, when these ability-based groups become permanent fixtures and when students are described by the leveled texts used in their guided reading groups. Permanent ability grouping can lead to lower expectations for less proficient readers, instead of seeing students as individuals (Boaler et al., 2000). Also, teachers are apt to focus on lower-level skills and strategies with lower-performing groups rather than engage students in high-level or critical discussions of texts (Du Plooy, 2019). Ability grouping also limits these students' access to more proficient readers, which deprives them of strong role models and demoralizes them along the way (Donnelly, 2019).

When teachers are not fully prepared to support student engagement across diverse genres of text, permanent ability grouping can also have the unintended consequence of identifying students by the leveled readers they use in guided reading groups, thereby limiting their access to materials that may be perceived as too challenging (Hoffman, 2017). There is an inherent tension between giving students books that are "just right" and having them identified by these levels—for instance, *You're a J-level reader. You should stick to those books.* Leveling is an effective tool if implemented in a way that does not limit students to only one "just right" level. Students should be able to choose books based on their interests, including ones that exhibit varied levels of complexity. Young and more mature readers should be shown how to navigate more complex books so they can be ready to take on more challenging reading material independently. Students are more likely to bring more sophisticated vocabulary to texts that reflect their interests and are incentivized to employ strategies for making sense of these texts.

Another potentially problematic literacy teaching practice involves questioning to monitor students' comprehension. Questions are distinguished by the degree to which they require complex thought to answer them. A low-level question, according to the revised Bloom's Taxonomy, is one that requires recalling and remembering information (Anderson & Krathwohl, 2001). Higher-level questioning prompts students to infer, analyze, evaluate, and create. Lower-level questioning tends to dominate in classrooms, a situation that deprives students of opportunities to thoughtfully grapple with complex ideas (Boyd & Markarian, 2011).

In addition, answers to low-level questions are often predetermined. Teachers have one correct answer in mind, the *known answer,* and a student's job is to identify it. This exchange is captured by the typical *initiation–response–evaluation* (IRE) discourse sequence known to many of us who have ever spent time in a classroom. The teacher initiates the sequence with a question (e.g., *Who is the main character?*), a student answers the question (*The main character is Johnny Tremain*), then the teacher evaluates the response (e.g., *Good job!* or *No; does someone else know?*). While such a sequence is designed to keep students focused and engaged, the problem is that when questions are presented to an entire class, often some portion of students raise their hands to answer, and one student is invited to respond. This leaves open questions about the number of students who are actually engaged in thinking about the text.

Another problem is whether students' individual and defensible interpretations of texts are being heard and honored (Aukerman & Chambers Schuldt, 2016). The tendency in classrooms is to get all students to agree on a teacher-favored, communal interpretation of a text. This can be problematic if students bring very different social and cultural experiences to texts than the ones that teachers or book authors bring. Students may have completely legitimate responses to texts, based on their own experiences, but their interpretations may not be supported by teachers or validated by book publishers (Dutro, 2009; Lewis, 1993).

We have touched on a handful of common teaching structures and routines that can potentially limit students' literacy growth. We don't need to rely entirely on the research to tell us what elements of literacy teaching are disengaging or intellectually stifling; we can just observe students. If students remain in the same ability groups for reading, they will acquire certain fixed identities about themselves as readers. If students hesitate to answer the teacher's questions because they see this as exposing what they don't know, they will be less engaged in the reading event. If they are rarely given opportunities to explore possible interpretations of texts in small, exploratory peer groups, their thoughts and opinions may be silenced. If they are given phonics instruction that is much too difficult or much too easy for them, they will either be frustrated or bored. The literacy classroom is a potential minefield of inequities, but it is the literacy teacher-advocate who can be vigilant about naming, noticing, and challenging them.

Pause and Reflect

1. In what ways do the structures and routines described in this chapter undermine the literacy growth or formation of literacy identities for students in your circles?
2. What would you need to do to become more vigilant about noticing and naming inequitable literacy teaching routines and structures?

DEFICIT DESCRIPTIONS AND APPROACHES

For many reasons, including their disproportionate representation in underfunded schools, students of color are continually undermined by deficit descriptions and approaches, which follow them beyond their exit from the K–12 education system. After Shoshanna graduated from her public high school in the Bronx, she moved on to attend a predominantly white institution (PWI) in upstate New York. Here she recalls attending the first day of her freshman seminar course:

> Our freshmen class was broken into seminar groups. On the first day of class, we had to go around the room and say who we were. And I said, "My name is Shoshanna. I'm from the Bronx." At the time, I was a pre-law student, I was a merit scholar, and I got a couple of regent scholarships, which I mentioned. After I spoke, it was time for people to ask me questions. The first student said, "Oh, so were you ever in a gang? And have you ever been shot?" That's what she got. That's what she got from me sharing all of these things about myself. It was just a really difficult transition at first because, you know, I realized that I had not lived the privilege that a lot of my classmates had.

Through the white gaze of her peers, Shoshanna and her world had been viewed at a deficit. Her college peers' racist remarks should serve as a constant reminder that the language that students and educators use can inflict harm and have a long-lasting impression. A frank conversation about the language we educators use is in order.

School hallways, teachers' lounges, and classrooms are loaded with deficit-laced terminology. Terms like "at-risk," "disadvantaged," "English Language Learner," and "Limited English Proficient" exemplify the deficit language that surrounds and inundates the lives of children from marginalized communities. Consider the latter phrases: English Language Learner and Limited English Proficient. They are both terms commonly used to designate students who are learning English. They are also labels that have wide-ranging consequences. The insinuation is that these students are *limited* or *lacking* as learners in some way, as if learning to speak two or more languages is a handicap. The American school system is very much backwards in this way of thinking, considering that almost half of the world's population is bilingual or multilingual, and that once they're older, speaking more than one language will give students a competitive advantage in college admissions, the job market, and communicating across linguistic communities. Still, our system discourages it, and that's a problem. We will delve deeper into issues of language in Chapter 5.

We have witnessed deficit talk about students' communities during our careers in education and social work. Here are just a few descriptors that are used for students' neighborhoods: "drug infested," "dangerous," "bad," "crime-ridden," "impoverished," and "ghetto." We hear these things all the time on our own college campus as teacher candidates will write or say: "That's a bad neighborhood." While we recognize that some Philadelphia zipcodes have higher crime rates than others, we also recognize the cultural wealth in economically stressed communities.

Patton et al. (2010) describe the kinds of cultural capital that their families and community members possessed while growing up in the primarily Black community of East St. Louis. These scholars presented several layers of wealth in communities of color that are oftentimes overlooked by cultural outsiders. These include social, familial, aspirational, navigational, and resistance forms of capital (Yosso, 2005), which we describe in Chapter 6. Not knowing about, let alone recognizing, these varied forms of capital leaves educators vulnerable to using deficit language about kids and their communities. This type of framing also provides a scapegoat for educational failure; believing that communities are failing kids lets educators off the hook for the problem.

Here's where it gets complicated. There is no doubt that poverty exerts a powerful effect on school literacy achievement (Allington, 2000). As we will see in Chapter 4, literacy practices within economically stressed homes and communities may look similar to those practiced in school, or they may look very different. For example, Purcell-Gates's (1996) study of 20 families with limited economic resources found great variability in their literacy experiences. She found that children in some families had 25 times more literacy engagements, such as reading books, than children in other families. Studies like these challenge the notion that literacy does not exist in homes located in economically distressed communities.

Yet the language that we hear some teacher candidates use when describing students' families can be categorized as deficit. In one study, teacher candidates indirectly accused caregivers of failing to provide either books or bedtime reading rituals, as reflected in this candidate's log entry: *I don't know what these students' home life is like, but if they are not being read to at home, this would be a reason why they aren't seeing and hearing reading as much and maybe struggling because of it* (Lazar, 2022, p. 169). This is why we invite teacher candidates to stop and think about what these comments really mean. We challenge them to explain how they could know about the literate lives of children if they are not engaged in round-the-clock investigative work to find out. Educators cannot make any assumptions about the literate lives of children unless they do serious ethnographic work in students' homes, schools, and communities across long periods of time. More fundamentally, we need to ask ourselves what good it does to make such assertions about students and their families.

Literacy classrooms also contain particular brands of deficit language. We have listened in as educators talk about the "low group," "Level B readers," "needy kids," "learning disabled students," and "slow" and "struggling" readers. Some use cute names for reading groups to distinguish between varied readers' abilities, for instance, the "triangle" group, the "purple" group, and so on. Children are not a reading level, nor are they a special-needs category. These deficit descriptions of children need to be jettisoned and replaced with descriptors that reflect kids' fullest capacities. Let's take a moment right now and think about this.

Pause and Reflect

1. Consider the language that you or others have used to describe students or families in economically distressed communities. How do our arguments about the need to refuse this language sit with you?
2. What forms of cultural capital have you noticed in your students' communities? Can you name them?
3. What humane, capacity-oriented language can you use to describe students and the lifestyles of families in economically stressed neighborhoods?

CONCLUSION

Understanding how a range of school factors make students vulnerable is an important part of becoming an advocacy-oriented teacher. High poverty rates, low levels of social supports for children's health and welfare, the unequal allocation of school resources, the resegregation of schools, inadequate systems for providing high-quality teachers, tracking practices in schools, and "factory-model school designs" contribute to vast discrepancies in educational opportunity, and those discrepancies disproportionately impact students of color (Darling-Hammond, 2015, p. 30). While it is not uncommon for educators to have thoughts like *I wish my students had more. . . . I wish they had a better teacher last year. . .* .this line of thinking, simply put, is just not helpful. If we approach our students in this way, what are we really saying to them? That we wish they were different? That we are blind to their strengths, talents, and genius? This is not the kind of messaging that inspires our students to see themselves as capable learners. We need to focus more on understanding the conditions that *positively,* not negatively, impact our students' lives. Next, we will look at issues of race and racism in the United States, because of their salience in the sociopolitical landscape of schooling and teaching.

Recommended Books

- *The Test: Why Our Schools Are Obsessed with Standardized Testing—But You Don't Have to Be* (Kamenetz, 2015)
- *Pushout: The Criminalization of Black Girls in Schools* (Morris, 2018)

- *A Wolf at the Schoolhouse Door: The Dismantling of Public Education and the Future of School* (Schneider & Berkshire, 2020)
- *Troublemakers: Lessons in Freedom from Young Children at School* (Shalaby, 2017)
- *Why Are All the Black Kids Sitting Together in the Cafeteria? And Other Conversations About Race* (Tatum, 2017)

CHAPTER 4

Racism in Schools and Society

> The saga of race in America is a tragic one—and it unfolds still.
>
> —Jon Meacham (2022)

Many of the elements that undermine students' literacy learning, as discussed in the last chapter, can be traced to structural racism. To understand structural racism, we need to take a step back and examine the nature of race, a construct that is complicated and often misunderstood. One of the most difficult parts of this work is acknowledging how we educators have been tainted by racist ideas and that our work going forward can either be one of noticing and dismantling racist schooling structures that undermine students' lives or ignoring them and becoming complicit in preserving white supremacy in our classrooms and schools. Some educators do not feel comfortable talking about race and racism, including with their students (Milner, 2017). Others want to talk about these issues with colleagues and students, but are either discouraged or prohibited from doing so.

In this chapter, we address some key ideas regarding race and systemic racism and how they are relevant to your role as an advocacy-focused teacher. There's no way we can do justice to topics like the history of race in America or how systemic racism is manifested today. Entire books are devoted to these topics—topics that may have been left out of the history courses you took in school. What we do is provide enough context about this scholarship to support our central point that knowing about racism is critical to dismantling it. At the end of this chapter, we offer suggestions for further reading so you can continue to learn about these topics, as part of your journey toward advocacy-focused teaching.

THE INVENTION OF RACE: A BRIEF HISTORY

Race is at once a *physical, social,* and *power* construct (Kendi, 2019; Milner, 2017), invented by people based on *phenotypes* (physical characteristics) for the primary purpose of economic exploitation. Race is also a *legal* and *historical* construct in that laws have been established to control the rights of people, thereby shaping their circumstances and opportunities throughout history in the United States and elsewhere (Milner, 2017). Race is also *contextual,* in that physical constructions of race differ across societies, regions, or countries. There are no gene markers that differentiate one group of humans from another. In addition, while racial categories such as Black, Latinx, and white exist, such racial categorizing is restrictive and regressive (Alim, 2016). Race is fluid as people choose to transcend fixed racial categories and *racially become* through language, actions, attitudes, preferences, and other modes of presentation (Reece, 2019). The word *racialized* describes the process of constructing racial categories to preserve the interests and power of the culturally dominant.

Racializing groups of people on the basis of skin color is a relatively recent invention in the course of human history. According to Ibram X. Kendi:

> For roughly two hundred thousand years, before race and racism were constructed in the fifteenth century, humans saw color but did not group the colors into continental races, did not commonly attach negative and positive characteristics to those colors and rank the races to justify racial inequity to reinforce racist power. (p. 236)

While the early notions of race came during European conquests of the Americas in the late 15th century, the human categorization that Kendi refers to occurred primarily in the 17th and 18th centuries, during the period commonly referred to as the Enlightenment. While the exact origin of the word *race* is disputed (Douglas & Ballard, 2008), European naturalists and philosophers of the day began to categorize humans. One of the first was Carl Linneas who initially divided humankind into four groups that corresponded with the then known continents: Europe, Asia, Africa, and America. He assigned each group a set of physical and character traits based on ideas established much earlier in time. Ancient Greek and Roman physicians and philosophers believed that the specific elements (air, water, fire, and earth) were associated with different climates and humors (blood, phlegm, yellow bile, and black bile). Linneas hypothesized that climate and geography influenced the presence of specific humors in people with particular skin tones and, further, that skin color correlated with specific character attributes (Jablonski, 2021). Other naturalists of the period studied relationships between skin color and climate (Buffon, 1853; Blumenbach, 1865), perpetuating the view that peoples' bodies and characters were inherently distinct based on their skin color.

Drawing upon these invented categories of race, philosophers Immanuel Kant and David Hume advanced the idea that humans could be categorized and hierarchically arranged by skin color, that skin color and moral character were linked, and that Europeans (whites) were superior to all other groups. Kant asserted that the hospitable temperate climate of Europe produced humans of high moral character and talent and that harsher climates were detrimental to the nature of those in other groups (Jablonski, 2021). The invented idea that Europeans were innately different from and superior to those of other groups was used to justify the transatlantic slave trade and the inhumane treatment of people of color.

THE IMPACT OF RACIAL CATEGORIZATIONS

Emerging ideas about racial groupings converged with economic activity in the colonization of the Americas. Throughout the 1600s, indentured servants from England and Ireland labored alongside other indentured and enslaved people of African ancestry. By 1676, Nathaniel Bacon led these allied groups to drive Native Americans out of Virginia, which resulted in the total destruction of Jamestown, Virginia (Geiter & Speck, 2002). This event, known as Bacon's Rebellion, unsettled wealthy landowners who were fearful of a multiracial alliance between laborers of African ancestry and their white counterparts. According to Michelle Alexander (2013), the planter elite "abandoned their heavy reliance on indentured servants in favor of the importation of more Black slaves" p. 24. Virginia landowners also passed laws that bestowed advantages to the laboring group that looked most like themselves—those with light skin tones (Berlin, 2003). They passed laws that guaranteed freedom and resources, like land, to those of European ancestry while instituting a system of permanent slavery for those of African ancestry. With these inducements, poor and indentured whites who had previously aligned with those of African ancestry, came to adopt the myth that they were superior to this group (Kelley, 2003). Not only did Virginia's leaders create unequal conditions between free whites and enslaved Africans, they also promoted whites' contempt for Africans, African Americans, and America's Indigenous people. This brief history shows how racial categories are inventions, created for social control and economic gain.

Property ownership and white supremacist structures are the basis of *settler colonialism*. Settler colonialism continues to work to systematically erase the presence of Indigenous people. Erasure of Indigenous people happens when folks say things like "William Penn founded Pennsylvania" or "Columbus discovered America"—as if no one existed on these lands prior to European colonization. Settler colonialism works through school curricula to either eliminate or gloss over certain ugly parts of our history, such as the Trail of Tears' mass removal and relocation of almost 100,000 Native people in the 1830s (Ehle, 1988), or the Indian boarding schools of the late 1800s and early 1900s that resulted in the near decimation of many Native peoples' languages and customs (Adams, 2020). Colonialism is upheld when we educators frame the westward expansion of European settlers across America as necessary for bringing democracy and capitalism from one shore to another, without critically examining the impact of this campaign on Native people who were forcibly removed from their ancestral lands. Failing to invite critical discussions about who gained and who lost in campaigns like Manifest Destiny will only preserve colonialist perspectives in schools.

We educators grapple with how to invite critical discussions about America, including its very establishment. Let's start with the truth. The truth is that from 1619 until the passage of the 13th Amendment of the U.S. Constitution in 1865, white landowners enslaved Blacks to produce cotton, tobacco, and rice for Southern-based industries (Harrison, 2021). The atrocities committed by white slave owners and overseers against the enslaved included brutal working conditions, selling and separating family members, rape, body branding, and routine beatings (Stubbs, 2018). In addition to carrying out these physical and psychological atrocities, whites instituted laws that denied the enslaved access to the written word. In many southern states, it was against the law to teach an enslaved person to read (Anele, 2020). The enslaved sought freedom from their bondage by engaging in many acts of resistance, including covertly learning to read, participating in slave revolts, and escaping via the Underground Railroad (Rodriguez, 2006). It took a Civil War that pitted the Union (North) against the southern slave-holding states to end human bondage in America. The Civil War ended in 1865, followed by a 12-year period of Reconstruction when the federal government intervened to reunify the United States and reconstitute governing bodies in the South.

Following Reconstruction, legalized racial segregation known as Jim Crow prevailed in much of the southern United States, restricting Blacks from voting, holding certain jobs, and owning property (Alexander, 2013). Jim Crow was strictly enforced in the South with separate public and private facilities for Blacks and whites, including water fountains, restrooms, and transportation. This time also gave rise to the Ku Klux Klan and their terror campaigns against Blacks, Roman Catholics, Jews, and foreigners (Parsons, 2019). Whites brutally attacked and murdered Black men and women in order to terrify and ultimately control them. Many lynchings were public spectacles, attended by whites in celebration of white supremacy (Wood, 2011).

During the Great Northern Migration (1910s through 1970), upwards of five million Black citizens fled the rural South and headed to northern, western, and midwestern cities in search of better opportunities. These new locations offered more of the same racially oppressive structures and institutions (Wilkerson, 2011). The government, under President Franklin D. Roosevelt, passed New Deal programs that systematically undermined Black citizens' ability to earn a decent wage and accumulate wealth. For example, the Fair Labor Standards Act (FLSA) provided a guaranteed minimum hourly wage and overtime pay to workers, but the law excluded domestic, agricultural, and tipped workers—many of whom were Black. "Congress intentionally excluded whole categories of workers from vital protections in order to deny Black people the opportunity for economic and social freedom and to preserve a system where employers could profit off of racist exploitation" (Dixon, 2021, p. 3). The government also passed homeownership legislation that resulted in the creation of maps to forecast home values. Those who designed these maps—white loan officers, appraisers, and real estate professionals—color-coded predominantly Black residential areas as red, indicating that these properties were likely to decrease in value. People living in *redlined* communities were often exempt from government insured mortgages, making home ownership out of reach for many (Almeida, 2021). The administration of the G.I. Bill also thwarted prospects for Black economic advancement. After World War II, Black veterans returning from the war were not afforded the same access to low-cost mortgages and business loans or higher education tuition assistance through the G.I. Bill that were given to white soldiers (Almeida, 2021). These and other government actions limited Black citizens' economic advancement, contributing to today's wealth gap between Black and white Americans. By 2016, the net worth of a typical white family was nearly 10 times greater than that of a typical Black family (McIntosh et al., 2020).

Black resistance to racially oppressive conditions mounted during the Civil Rights Era of the 1950s and 1960s. In 1954, the U.S. Supreme Court ruled that racial segregation in public schools was unconstitutional in the *Brown v. Board of Education* case. The passage of *Brown* did not mean that white citizens would comply with it. It took major federal intervention for Black students to integrate schools. The first test of the law came in Little Rock, Arkansas, when nine African American students enrolled in the town's public high school. The students were initially barred from attending by Arkansas Governor Orval Faubus, but President Dwight Eisenhower intervened and the students were finally able to attend—not without major resistance by white segregationists (Anderson, 2013). President Eisenhower called in the U.S. infantry and the U.S. Marshals Service to keep order and escort the nine students into and out of the school building while angry white mobs screamed and some even threated to lynch students. A few years later in 1960, 6-year-old Ruby Bridges was the youngest child to integrate an all-white elementary school in New Orleans. She entered the school while crowds of white people yelled slurs and waved racist placards at her.

Appropriating Martin Luther King Jr.'s teachings of nonviolent resistance, many Black activists protested peacefully in the face of beatings, police dogs, fire hoses, and jail in order to fight for racial equality in schools and other public spaces. These acts inspired massive demonstrations for racial justice, which set in motion resistance by other oppressed groups—including women. These demonstrations became hallmark events of the Civil Rights Era. Martin Luther King Jr. made his famous "I Have a Dream" speech in Washington, D.C., in 1963, creating a moral imperative that led to the passage of the Civil Rights Act of 1964. This legislation prohibited discrimination on the basis of race, color, religion, sex, or national origin. Even though the Act did more to provide equal treatment to African Americans, the dream of racial justice has never been fully realized. Neither the *Brown* decision nor the Civil Rights Act of 1964 could stop subsequent decades of de facto segregation that occurred as white people fled integrated communities and fought forced integration attempts such as the busing of Black students into predominantly white schools. School integration peaked in the 1970s and 1980s but it has since eroded due to lack of enforcement. In 2020–2021, about one third of American public school students attended a school predominantly populated by their own race or ethnicity (Government Accounting Office, 2022).

The premise behind school integration was to equalize educational opportunities by giving Black students access to the better funded educational facilities provided in predominantly white communities. Let's stop, however, to consider what was lost due to school integration legislation. While buildings and learning resources for Blacks were historically meager compared with those afforded to white people, social networks within the Black community sustained Black students' learning. According to Vanessa Siddle Walker (1996), "Although Black schools were indeed commonly lacking in facilities and funding, some evidence suggests that the environment of the segregated school had affective traits, institutional policies and community support that helped Black children learn in spite of the neglect their schools received from white school boards" (p. 3). In addition, efforts to desegregate schools left thousands of African American teachers out of jobs, which meant that Black students had less access to teachers who looked like them, advocated for them, or championed their success.

Civil rights legislation of the 1960s never erased systemic racism because discriminatory policies continue to advantage whites and disadvantage people of color. Since discriminatory policies are a root cause of systemic racism, the more precise term *policy racism* is warranted (Kendi, 2019). Policy/systemic racism limits equal access to a range of sectors including voting, police protection, housing, health care, the judicial system, and education. Recognizing racism as a systemic or policy problem, and not just as a problem of individuals mistreating each other, is the basis of *critical race theory (CRT)*, a concept we will approach next. Let's stop here for a moment and reflect.

Pause and Reflect

1. How have you been taught to think about race?
2. Why does it make sense that race can be considered *power* and *policy* constructs and not just a *social* one?
3. For much of your life, segregation has been illegal. In what ways has racial segregation continued?

MISINTERPRETING CRITICAL RACE THEORY AND THE NEED TO ADDRESS RACISM IN SCHOOL

CRT is a multilayered concept developed in the 1970s by legal scholars to explain the persistence of racial disparities in the United States despite the civil rights reforms of the 1950s and 1960s (Bell, 1980, 1995; Crenshaw et al., 1995; Delgado, 1984; Matsuda, 1991). CRT theorists hold that racism is baked into the structures, policies, and institutions of American society, and as such, it operates persistently to undermine the life opportunities of people of color. Racism is a common experience for most people of color in America, and its ordinariness makes it difficult to identify and acknowledge. Colorblindness ensures that people overlook and disregard how white supremacy works in institutions and structures to systematically disadvantage people of color. Videos and personal testimonies serve as powerful evidence of the existence of systemic racism. For instance, the video of George Floyd's murder, and the testimonies of those who witnessed it, provided powerful evidence of racial discrimination and excessive force by members of the Minneapolis Police Department. This finding triggered many city officials across the country to examine racial injustices in their policing policies and practices.

Another dimension of CRT is the idea of interest convergence, the notion that white people will support racial equality when it furthers their goals and interests. Since "racism advances the interests of both white elites (materially) and working-class whites (psychically), large segments of society have little incentive to eradicate it" (Delgado & Stefancic, 2017, p. 9). Derrick Bell (1980) used the 1954 *Brown v. Board of Education* Supreme Court decision to end school segregation as an example of interest convergence. This decision was supported by the white elite who wanted to prove to the world that America treated all of its citizens fairly as tensions between the United States and the Soviet Union escalated after World War II.

In addition, CRT addresses the idea that race is a social construction, a concept we addressed at the beginning of this chapter. "People with common origins share certain physical traits, of course, such as skin color, physique, and hair texture. But these constitute only an extremely small portion of their genetic endowment, are dwarfed by what we have in common, and have little or nothing to do with distinctly human, higher-order traits, such as personality, intelligence, and moral behavior" (Delgado & Stefancic, 2017, p. 9). Racial categories were invented by white people to oppress and exploit people of color.

CRT theorists explore how systemic racism impacts members of different racialized communities. LatCrit, for instance, is a field of study that focuses on the ways that Latinx-affiliating groups are subjugated by elements like discriminatory immigration laws and restrictive language policies in schools and institutions. This body of scholarship is distinct from TribalCrit, which focuses on issues that hold particular significance to Indigenous people, such as colonization and cultural decimation. CRT scholars also address issues of intersectionality and the ways individuals experience subjugation based on their multiple identity affiliations. As such, CRT takes a strong anti-essentialist position in that "no person has a single, easily stated, unitary identity" (Delgado & Stefancic, 2017 p. 10) and therefore no person experiences subjugation in exactly the same way as another.

CRT is not in any way, shape, or form, a school-based curriculum. No elementary school teacher we know teaches CRT. You are not going to find CRT listed in any elementary school curriculum guide. Discussions of CRT are typically located in graduate-level university programs. When teachers discuss the unfair treatment of BIPOC communities in history or contemporary life, they are not teaching the theoretical construct of CRT. Claiming that CRT is being taught to children is a political scare tactic designed to eradicate *any* mention of racism in schools. Some folks believe the topic of racism should be off limits to children because it teaches white children to feel guilty and ashamed of themselves, and that children of color will feel resentful toward white children. The fact is, children are bombarded by messages about racism and white supremacy through various media outlets.

Children witness blatant acts of racism on television. Recall when white nationalists chanted "Jews will not replace us" while they marched in Charlottesville, Virginia, in 2017. How did children absorb this message? On May 2022, an 18-year-old white supremacist entered a grocery store in Buffalo, New York, and killed 13 people—11 Black and 2 white—using a semiautomatic rifle. How did children interpret this event? As educators, we need to talk about these blatant forms of white supremacy; we need to discuss forms of systemic racism that are deeply woven into U.S. history and continue to deny people of color basic rights and opportunities. Unfortunately, the climate for talking about these issues has changed radically over the last few years. There has been a full pendulum shift and more and more educators are having to question: "Am I 'allowed' to talk about these events?" To this we ask: *Is silence here not complicity? Is it not how the 18-year-old in Buffalo ended up live streaming a racially motivated mass murder?* What we recognize is that the waters are turbulent and educators are finding themselves rocked by the "cans" and the "cannots." Kaitlin discusses the weight local educators feel as they teach in the current climate:

> James, one of my graduate students, is a full-time middle school teacher in a suburban school district. He recently commented that navigating any discussion of identity in the classroom right now feels like constructing a plane in flight . . . and changing the model from a single-engine Cessna to a 747 . . . then changing it back again. The rhetoric and fear of surveillance is unsettling. In his "purple" political community, politicians and (mostly) white parents are very loudly vilifying CRT, which he feels is really just a scapegoat for any visible

> approach to diversity, equity, and inclusion. Their argument goes that parents want to raise their children to not see differences, and they don't want their children to feel bad about who they are or where they come from. Like many educators, James is feeling the force, and velocity, of an anti-diversity/equity/inclusion pendulum that has swung to the right. It puts an educator like him, who wants to engage in activist work, in a very difficult spot. It's hard to be a teacher advocate for change when you're out of a job.

Many state legislators around the United States have either passed laws or are proposing laws to squelch school discussions about the history of racism and how racism is manifested today. At the time of this writing, several states have either passed or introduced legislation that prohibits teachers from discussing issues of race or racial injustice (Sachs, 2022). Florida's Stop WOKE Act, backed by Governor Ron DeSantis, prevents educators from teaching in ways that provoke students' feelings of "discomfort, guilt, anguish, or any other form of psychological distress on account of his or her race, color, sex, or national origin" (Vile, 2022). How does one teach about American enslavement without mentioning the atrocities committed by white slave owners and overseers? How does one teach about the Ku Klux Klan without mentioning how whites lynched and terrorized thousands of Black people? How does one teach about Jim Crow without mentioning that white people established and preserved segregation laws?

We need to understand that children already bring knowledge about racism to classrooms and have the capacity to study justice and inequality in their own and others' lives. One study of 2nd-graders who responded to historical literature that addressed racism (Rogers & Mosley, 2006) found that white students simultaneously noticed and enacted whiteness, and in some cases, disrupted the idea of white privilege and indicated they would fight for racial equality. The experience enabled children to "step into texts to identify, problematize, and, most importantly, construct whiteness in relation to social justice" (p. 483). Another study (Wegrzyn, 2022) looked at white and Brown identifying 5th-graders in an after-school program who read and responded to the book *Stamped (for Kids), Racism, Antiracism and You* (Cherry-Paul et al., 2021). After participating in the program, students critiqued their prior educational experiences that denied them opportunities to explore and grapple with questions about racism. In addition, these children wanted to continue to learn more about racism and the experiences of people of color after the program ended. These studies do not support the idea that discussions about race and racism make children feel bad about themselves. On the contrary, it describes their willingness to engage in discussions about story characters who display racist, activist, and ally stances and their curiosity about the ways racism has functioned in history and how it continues to operate in contemporary life.

Laws like Florida's Stop WOKE Act are making it possible for parents and literally anyone in the community to report on teachers who discuss racism. Our colleagues in Florida report panic among teachers who are afraid to talk about anything that might be controversial. Many are now covering their classroom libraries with signs that say "Books Not Available" until media specialists determine the appropriateness of each text. While the level of surveillance of classrooms has ratcheted up considerably, teachers and school leaders have demonstrated a range of reactions, from compliance to resistance.

If this truth-suppressionist movement gains momentum, it will prevent massive numbers of students from learning facts about U.S. history or present-day racially motivated murders, attacks, or disparities of access or opportunity. *Not teaching* about these ugly truths is a recipe for ignorance, which fuels bigotry and preserves systemic racism. Althier recalls her own public schooling experience and the consequences of being kept ignorant about systemic racism:

> There were no conversations about racial injustice while attending my nearly all-white high school in Massachusetts in the 1970s, even though race-based rioting played out nightly on the news. Angry white South Boston parents screamed into television cameras about their kids being bused to the predominantly Black Roxbury High School. I saw white teens throwing bottles and rocks at school buses. While this was going on, the teachers at my school were silent about the school busing riots. There were no classroom discussions about unequal schooling or why school desegregation laws existed or how we might take a stand on this issue. Silence. It took decades of self-study to come to grips with systemic racism and see my place in it. If only this conversation had been jump-started in my youth.

Beyond ignorance, the consequences of silence are deadly. Keeping students in the dark about racism will ensure that racially motivated murders like the one carried out at Tops Friendly Market in Buffalo in 2022 will continue, and organizations like the Proud Boys will have plenty of future recruits. It is absurd to think that we educators would be expected to keep historical truths from students. In Chapter 5 we discuss critical literacy as a mechanism for using texts to talk about racism and for shaping students' identities as anti-racists.

PAUSE AND REFLECT

1. Search online to investigate how critical race theory is being discussed and interpreted in your state/region.
2. What efforts are underway to curb the way teachers address racism, or forms of subjugation other than race?

LITERACY EDUCATOR ACTIVISM: NOTICING, QUESTIONING, CHALLENGING

Now that we've laid a modest foundation for understanding the roots of systemic/policy racism and inequity, we are left with the problem of what to do about it. After studying and acknowledging the existence of systemic inequities in schools and society, many of our teachers and teacher candidates feel powerless to do anything about it. They say: *What can I do? I don't have any power to change schools!* We know that you alone may not have the power to make big changes in your school at this very moment, but we believe teachers, principals, and other school administrators can work together to make decisions that lead to equitable educational outcomes for kids.

What is needed is engagement and the will to accept responsibility for the inequities that are happening *now*. Engagement, however, has its challenges in this social and political climate. Kaitlin shares her experience working with teacher candidates over the last year:

> The national conversation around race seems to be more dominant than ever, but I have found that engaging preservice students in open, honest, and at times raw discussions has grown more difficult over the last few years. My white students, in particular, are hyper aware of getting "canceled." They are listening, which is extremely important, and they've privately shared with me a desire to authentically engage, discuss, and discern in a classroom setting, but they find themselves constantly questioning if they're saying the "wrong" thing, using the "wrong" words, causing any kind of hurt or harm, and/or offending BIPOC persons in any way. The fear is that if they bungle a thought, misuse a word, or show the class that they're not as far along in doing the work, they'll be canceled—or, worse, labeled a racist. As a white person, I can relate to these feelings, but I also understand that staying quiet isn't productive. As an educator and a leader, I'm troubled by the lack of safe spaces for growth in our classrooms along the white identity continuum when it comes to talking about race.

To make progress in understanding racism, we've got to create spaces to talk about how it came to be and how it is manifested now. When we talk about accepting responsibility, we mean seeing, naming, and challenging racial injustices that happen in schools and elsewhere (Kendi, 2019).

For teachers, it's about connecting the dots between students' racial affiliations and their opportunities to access equitable schooling opportunities. This is the hard part because racism has become so normalized that it is difficult to see. But when you actively study the history and current realities of racial injustice, patterns start to emerge. You can start now by noticing and naming instances of inequity right in front of you, in your own school. *Does it seem like disproportionate numbers of Black and Latinx kids get suspended in your school? Do the children appear disinterested or unengaged when you follow the district's curriculum guide? Do students get ranked and sorted within and across classrooms based on high-stakes tests? Do some children get left out of gifted programs because the assessments being used to determine their eligibility are racially or culturally biased?*

Questions like these are only the beginning. What we need to do is follow each question to a policy or a decision that a person or group made somewhere along the line. We can ask: *How are curriculum decisions made? Who makes them? How was it decided that students should spend inordinate amounts of time preparing for standardized tests? How is it that children of color are tracked into certain classes on the basis of high-stakes test scores?* You cannot do this kind of inquiry work alone. Working with others to find the answers to these questions is part of the advocacy work that needs to be done to make our schools more equitable.

Asking questions about why things are the way they are is the first part of advocacy. The second part is calling out and challenging patterns of injustice. *White allies* are white individuals who show support to people of color, but there's a big difference between showing support and advocacy. According to Bettina Love (2019), being an ally is different from being a *co-conspirator*. Co-conspirators not only support anti-racist causes, but are willing to sacrifice their freedom or even their lives to do it. Love uses the example of James Tyson, a white activist who assisted African American activist Bree Newsome as she took down the Confederate flag that hung at South Carolina's state house grounds in 2015. Newsome took this action just days after 21-year-old white supremacist Dylann Roof shot and killed nine people during a Bible study at Charleston's African Methodist Episcopal Church. Roof had posted racist messages on his website and pictures of himself holding a handgun and a Confederate flag, which led to protests over the presence of the flag at the state house. Tyson stood at the base of the flagpole to spot Newsome as she climbed. Realizing that police were about to use a taser to get her down from the pole, which could have killed her, Tyson held onto the pole knowing that the police would not use tasers if he, a white man, held onto it. After Newsome climbed down from the pole, both she and Tyson were arrested. Newsome was the one credited for taking down the flag, while Tyson, her white co-conspirator, leveraged the power of his whiteness to help her succeed.

What do co-conspirator educators look like? What does an advocacy-focused teacher look like? To begin with, it looks like *understanding*. It means understanding what many families of color have been up against historically, socially, and politically. If you understand these things, then you will not blame caregivers for what are actually the shortcomings of educational and societal systems. Being an advocate means linking arms with caregivers and learning from them. It means studying the heritage and experiences of families. It means understanding the various forms of cultural capital that they bring to school and drawing from this bank of cultural knowledge to inform your instruction. It means setting high expectations for students and providing the scaffolds and culturally welcoming curricula they need to meet these expectations. It means recognizing a practice like culturally unfair tests and banding together with other teachers to challenge the use of these tests at a school board meeting. Bringing these elements to your literacy teaching practice is a form of political action.

Understanding also involves listening to students' stories of disengagement and asking whether we've done enough to make our schools the culturally affirming places they deserve to be. Many educators try to make schools culturally affirming by doing things like hanging up posters of Martin Luther King Jr. or Rosa Parks. There's nothing wrong with this, but it doesn't go far enough in creating a culturally affirming school. Celebrating Black History Month only reinforces the notion that these activists and the achievements of people of color are somehow separate from U.S. history and not really integral to the school experience. Staging a "heritage day" where students' families are invited to bring cultural artifacts and dishes from their home countries is a warm and fuzzy idea, but again, it is confined to the margins of the academic calendar. Not questioning the place of Black History Month in the curriculum and taking an uncritical stance about "culture day" are just two out of thousands of ways that we educators are preserving the structure of white supremacy in schools. Being an *abolitionist* teacher means asking how we can affirm students' cultural heritage and experiences by placing them at the center of schooling, not at the periphery. To advocate in these ways, we must first do the serious internal work of exploring how issues of race and culture live inside all of us, as we discussed in Chapter 2.

PAUSE AND REFLECT

1. Name some of the ways students in your school or field placement are being denied access to high-quality literacy learning opportunities. How do you think these opportunities have been historically shaped?
2. How is one of these ways linked to a school policy, district guideline, or curriculum mandate?

CONCLUSION

In this chapter, we have touched on the human invention of race, how racism has manifested in U.S. history, and how it continues to work today to advantage white people and disadvantage people of color. We can take away from this history a disheartened sense of the inhumanity of white people and the victimization of people of color. Don't. History is much more complicated. Many white allies and co-conspirators have been willing to sacrifice their lives and liberty for racial justice. Likewise, Black and Native American history is not about victimization. It is about resilience, resistance, ingenuity, creativity, faith, and community. Please accept our invitations to explore more history. At the end of this chapter, we have left you with a short list of highly recommended books. Developing a richer sense of history will help you establish your place in challenging the injustices of today, including the latest wave to restrict what books teachers can use and what they can say in order to make some white folks feel more comfortable.

We have a choice to make. We can either keep our students blind to the history of race and realities of systemic racism and ensure that they preserve racial inequities, or we can explore these realities in our classrooms and take a stand against white supremacy. It's not about making white kids feel guilty. It's about encouraging young students to inquire about the world as it really is and consider the ways its current problems might be solved. In the next chapter, we will address the varied and legitimate literacies and languages that our students bring to our classrooms and the implications of judging students according to school-valued literacies and languages.

Recommended Books

- *The New Jim Crow: Mass Incarceration in the Age of Colorblindness* (Alexander, 2020)
- *An Indigenous Peoples' History of the United States* (Dunbar-Ortiz, 2015)
- *The 1619 Project: A New Origin Story* (Hannah-Jones, 2021)
- *Stamped from the Beginning: The Definitive History of Racist Ideas in America* (Kendi, 2016)
- *Lies My Teacher Told Me: Everything American History Books Get Wrong* (Loewen, 2019)
- *How the Word Is Passed: A Reckoning with the History of Slavery in America* (Smith, 2021)
- *Caste: The Origins of Our Discontents* (Wilkerson, 2023)
- *A People's History of the United States* (Zinn, 2015)

CHAPTER 5

Many Literacies and Languages

> Acknowledging the importance of students' language and literacy skill development in their very early years of life, educators may set Black students up for failure when they refuse to recognize or do not have the frames to identify language and literacy assets, strengths, skills, dispositions, mind-sets, and practices that these students already possess and bring into a classroom.
>
> —H. Richard Milner IV (2020, p. S250)

RETHINKING PERSPECTIVES ABOUT LITERACY AND LANGUAGE

For students who speak marginalized varieties of English, and those whose primary language is not English, schools can be hostile and alienating places (Baker-Bell, 2020; García & Kleifgen, 2018). Students who show up to the kindergarten classroom lacking a predetermined set of literacy skills are often deemed inadequate, slow, or at-risk when they enter school (Milner, 2020), and some educators have been quick to blame caregivers for failing to enculturate their children to school-valued ways of using spoken and printed language. Educators may not recognize their involvement in such shaming and blaming, or how these incidents erode students' identities and their connection to school. Too many educators have not had opportunities to examine their assumptions about students' literacies and languages and so we see this as a space for educator growth.

In U.S. schools, expectations for literacy development have been traditionally molded around the lifestyles and knowledge traditions of the culturally dominant, with roots in European (white), English-speaking literary and linguistic traditions (Anyon, 2014; Heath, 1983). Book reading and essay writing are two types of school-valued literacy practices. Caregivers may enculturate their children in these practices through rituals like collecting books, engaging in bedtime reading, and asking children to describe their experiences or defend their opinions. If you are obtaining a teacher's license, or already have one, you probably grew up in a home with caregivers who apprenticed you in the kinds of reading, writing, and talking practices that prepared you to do well in school. Or, maybe you did not grow up in a home with these school-valued literacies, but you learned them from teachers or others in your community. The idea is that you developed the school-valued literacies required to become an educator.

Now try to put yourself in the shoes of kindergarteners whose home literacies and languages look quite different from those valued in schools. Instead of books, your home is filled with singing, storytelling, art posters, bus schedules, comic books, text messaging, and Instagram—all literacies, but not the kinds of reading and book-discussion literacies that are prioritized in schools. Let's also imagine that you know some English and a lot of Spanish and often find yourself translating for your Spanish-speaking parents. You can draw very elaborate pictures and tell fanciful stories, but your teacher determines that you are academically behind because you are mostly silent in class and have not yet learned the alphabet. You are given lots of letter-tracing and copying work to do. Your teacher does not invite you to describe the pictures that you draw by using the letters or words that you know. The stories your teacher reads aloud to the class contain characters and events that seem unfamiliar. Sometimes she stops and asks questions about these stories, but you are not familiar with these types of questions and worry that if you open your mouth, the words might come out wrong. Once, the teacher called on you and you did not know the answer. It was embarrassing. Midway through the school year, your teacher leaves for a higher paying job and you get another teacher fresh out of college. You do more worksheets. Some of your classmates are starting to read books. As you start 1st grade, you are considered a full year behind your peers academically. Your teacher describes you as a "slow learner," and you begin to think you are.

If you can imagine yourself as this child, then you are one step closer to understanding how some kids experience school when their literacies and languages are misjudged. Let's imagine a very different scenario.

Before school opens in the fall, your teacher arranges a meeting with your caregivers, with a translator present, to find out more about your family and the kinds of things you do at home. Imagine that she invites you to speak both Spanish and English in school. Instead of copying letters, she teaches you to label your pictures, and eventually you are able to write sentence-length captions under your pictures. She invites you to write your captions in both Spanish and English. She displays your stories on the classroom walls so that those students who only know English can also learn Spanish. Your teacher welcomes multilingual parent helpers to come to the classroom and uses Google Translate to help students write in English and Spanish. Your teacher decides that you and your peers are ready to showcase your bilingual stories. She asks you to write a bilingual invitation to welcome the 1st-graders into your class. You feel proud to be a writer, illustrator, and teacher. Your teacher also brings stories into your class that reflect some of the things your family does and some of the ways they say things. You love these stories and listen closely. You are comfortable taking risks answering the teacher's questions about the books she reads aloud. Your teacher also brings lots of songs into class, including songs that help you remember the kinds of sounds that go with certain letters and letter combinations. She prepares a packet of letters and their sounds that is just right for you and makes sure there is time every day for phonics study. She lets you pronounce certain letters your way and in a way that others understand. Your teacher makes books available for you to read at home, not just after school but all summer long. These books include both English and Spanish, with characters and experiences that remind you of the things you do at home. Sometimes the characters even say things that seem familiar. You are excited to go to 1st grade.

These starkly different visions of literacy and language teaching communicate the difference between what school is often like for kids whose literacies and languages are dismissed and denigrated, and what school could be—a place that builds on the literacies and languages that all learners bring to school and fosters a trajectory of literacy success for all kids. We can do this work. We can cultivate critical understandings of how literacies and languages are perceived and treated in school. We can interrogate the assumption that acquiring school-valued academic literacies will ensure that students pass standardized tests, compose coherent essays, get into college, and secure jobs. We can develop wonder-filled and awestruck orientations to students' ways with words and print (Bomer, 2010). We will begin by examining some concepts that are grounded in ethnographic studies of communities' use of literacies and languages.

AUTONOMOUS AND IDEOLOGICAL CONCEPTIONS OF LITERACY REVISITED

Many educators tend to see school-valued literacies as normal and valuable and the ones that should define what it means to be literate. An *autonomous* view of literacy (Street, 1984) holds that there is one specific, discrete, normative, and politically neutral set of literacy practices (book reading, learning the alphabet, writing essays, etc.) that are disconnected from culture and must be mastered in order for someone to be considered literate. If school-valued literacies are the only ones that count in school, then teachers will assume that students who do poorly on school assignments and standardized tests have not been exposed to literacy within their homes. The reality is that literacy and language are *culturally situated practices*. This means they are practiced in social communities and are therefore shaped by the values, understandings, needs, and goals of people in particular cultural communities. There is no such thing as one kind of literacy or language. There are many literacies and languages used by different communities for specific purposes. All are legitimate.

If we do not accept the premise that all literacies are culturally situated and legitimate, then we are bound to misjudge students. We might even hear these types of comments whirling around the teacher's lounge: *There's no literacy going on in that home. They don't read to their kids! They have no books in that house!* Educators say these things as if book reading is a practice that all families are supposed to engage in. These statements reflect an autonomous view of literacy.

Alternatively, we can hold an *ideological* view of literacy (Street, 1984), which maintains that literacy and culture are inseparable. Literacy and language are cultural practices that serve specific communicative purposes. For instance, double Dutch rope jumping, hand-clapping rhymes, call and response, spoken word poetry, playing the dozens, gospels, spirituals, and hip-hop music are all ways of using literacy and language that are rooted in the Black experience, reflecting the linguistic versatility of its members and the use of words to assert identities and counter white oppression (Greene, 2020; Kinloch et al., 2020; Muhammad & Haddix, 2016; Price-Dennis & Muhammad, 2021). An ideological view forces us to rethink and question what literacy is and does and for whom.

A BIT OF HISTORY: THE HEATH STUDY

Shirley Brice Heath (1982) studied the ways families used language and print in three communities in a southeast region of the United States: Maintown, Roadville, and Trackton. Heath found that the language socialization patterns of these communities differed dramatically from each other, with consequences for adjusting to and succeeding in school.

Maintown represented a school-oriented culture of professionally educated caregivers who read to their children at bedtime and engaged in school-like conversations about texts. While reading stories aloud, caregivers asked questions that prompted children to label two-dimensional illustrations of real objects (*What's that? Is that a picture of a dog?*). These ways of talking about texts prepared children for the "initiation–response–evaluation" sequences that are typically used by teachers in schools. Maintown caregivers also engaged in elaborated talk about texts that required children to give reason-explanations to why questions (*Why did the character do that?*) and affective commentaries (*Why do you think the character did the right thing?*). These literacy socialization patterns were consistent with school literacy expectations, preparing Maintown students for school success. This was not the case for students in the other two communities.

The white, working-class parents of Roadville talked directly to their infants and prompted their toddlers to name objects around the house. They read stories aloud for a few minutes at night, but did not invite children to imagine themselves as characters or engage in elaborate conversations about texts. Children were expected to tell the truth and avoid fanciful storytelling. Roadville schoolchildren met school literacy expectations in the early primary grades, but their home literacy practices did not prepare them for the kinds of higher-order literacy engagements needed for later school success. These children could retell stories, but had difficulty creating their own. They had difficulty analyzing texts or answering hypothetical questions that related story characters or events to possible novel situations. By the 4th grade, many of these children had difficulty keeping up with the literacy expectations of school.

The African American caregivers in the mill town of Trackton did not perceive their infants as suitable conversation partners, but instead enveloped their babies in a constant stream of adult talk and storytelling. Toddlers repeated bits of the language they had heard and, as they became more verbally adept, young children found ways to enter into adult conversations. Heath reported that the types of questions that adults used with children included analogy-type questions (*What's that like?*), story-starter questions (*Did you see Maggie's dog?*) and accusation-questions (*What's that all over your face?*). Since children were not seen as information givers, adults tended not to ask very young children questions—especially those they already knew the answers to. As they grew, children were encouraged to tell stories about their experiences and lived situations. Boys were especially recognized by their ability to hold an audience through their storytelling abilities. Trackton caregivers kept very few books outside of the Bible and school books, but homes contained an array of print such as newspapers, mail, brochures, advertisements, product labels, and church materials. The adults in this community did not intentionally demonstrate to their children how to read, but children had many opportunities to engage in reading or writing by observing adults and older peers read or write for specific purposes such as paying bills, shopping for groceries, or writing letters. Reading was often a social activity as adults read aloud while others commented on and negotiated the meanings of texts based on their own experiences. When children from Trackton entered school, they were not familiar with the kinds of labeling tasks or questions that are typically used in the early grades. Nor were they familiar with how to sit and listen to stories read aloud and respond to teachers' known-answer questions. The higher-level literate capacities they had developed in their communities were not tapped within the school curriculum.

The biggest takeaway from Heath's research is the need to understand school literacy achievement as a function of the degree of match between school expectations and families' ways of using spoken and printed language. The greater the match, the more likely it is that students will achieve. Her findings also indicated that school literacy failure is a consequence of ignoring or dismissing families' ways of using language. There may be children in your classroom who are floundering on standardized literacy tests or who do not want to sit quietly to listen to books being read aloud because *they might not have been socialized to engage in these activities.* Here's the important thing though—*we cannot assume that this is the case.*

CRITIQUING THE "WORD GAP" RESEARCH

In the mid-1990s, researchers Betty Hart and Todd Risley published a controversial study of contrasting linguistic and academic progress among children from different socioeconomic backgrounds. Specifically, they studied how daily communication between parent and child shape language and vocabulary development, and how a family's economic status might play a role in that development. Though they only studied 42 families, Hart and Risley proposed that children from high-income families were exposed to 30 million more words than children from ones receiving government financial assistance—a disparity that came to be known as "the 30-million-word gap" (Hart & Risley, 1995). Of the 42 families, only 29 families were followed into elementary school. Based on the Hart and Risley study, programs such as *Providence Talks* have been launched to address the "word gap" of children in "disadvantaged families" (Borg, 2015). In Providence Talks, family conversations are recorded and studied and trainers are sent to help caregivers boost the number of words they use with their children.

Findings from Hart and Risley's study have been refuted by Douglas Sperry and his colleagues (Sperry et al., 2019). They looked at a similar number of families, but researchers who entered these homes spent time getting to know the communities and the study participants before the study took place. Sperry et al. found no word gap differences between lower and higher income families, and instead "found some poor and working-class communities showed an advantage in the number of words children heard, compared with middle-class communities" (p. 1313). For instance, they found that the African American children in the community named "Poor Black Belt" had a higher number of words spoken to them than the children tagged as poor, middle-, and working-class European American. Despite results from the Sperry et al. study, policies and programs continue to chase the flawed premise of the Hart and Risley study, which suggests that the language experiences of low-income families of color are deficient and need to be reformed. Viewing family literacy practices through a deficit lens not only results in pathologizing students as "at-risk," but it communicates to caregivers that something must be inherently wrong with their children, as Milner (2020) states:

> Rather than helping families understand that reading skills (e.g., processing speed) can be and usually are enhanced over time, Black families may get the message that something is innately wrong with their children because they

> do not fall within a "normal" reading/testing distribution. It is important to note that Black families' interpretation of such labels may be qualitatively different from that of white families because (covertly and overtly) Black people receive the message that their children are inferior and must catch up or keep up with their white counterparts (Ladson-Billings, 2006) without any interrogation of the ways in which racism and other forms of structural oppression maintain an inequitable status quo in the policies and practices of schooling. (p. 250)

We educators need to broaden our understanding of literacy. If literacies are varied, purposeful, and communicative cultural practices, then literacy is certainly more than just book reading and essay writing. Literacy, as defined by the National Council of Teachers of English, "is the way that we interact with the world around us, how we shape it and are shaped by it. It is how we communicate with others via reading and writing, but also by speaking, listening, and creating" (NCTE, 2020). This means that family songs, Instagram photos, spray-painted subway cars, self-help blogs, recipes, testimonials, sermons, scrapbooks, and podcasts would all be *forms of literacy*. The question is—in what ways do we educators see and welcome the literacies that are used by our students, their families, and their communities?

PAUSE AND REFLECT

1. Take time to remember your own family's ways of using spoken and printed language. How were these ways consistent or inconsistent with the literacy/language expectations of school?
2. How can you find out more about the literacy/language practices that students bring to your classroom? What might you ask their caregivers to share with you?

ENGLISHES, RACIOLINGUISTICS, AND CODE-MESHING

Next we will focus on ideological and inclusive stances toward students' language, particularly regarding students who, along with their families, speak varied forms of English (Smith, 2020). Many who identify as Black in the United States use features of Black Language (BL) (Baker-Bell, 2020), which is rooted in English and West African linguistic traditions (Charity Hudley & Mallinson, 2010; Smith, 2020). We need, however, to recognize the variation across different ethno-racial communities in speakers' use of English. In the Philadelphia area, for example, recent newcomer students from the West Indies, many originating from Haiti, speak a type of English with roots in French-based Creole, whereas those from Jamaica speak varieties of English with Jamaican Patois roots. These Englishes are distinct from those used by students originating from Liberia, Nigeria, or other West African nations.

Speakers of marginalized Englishes face different types of restrictions and denigration. April Baker-Bell (2020) describes the harm that many Black Language speakers experience in school as a form of linguistic violence:

> Anti-Black linguistic racism refers to the linguistic violence, persecution, dehumanization, and marginalization that Black Language (BL) speakers endure when using their language in schools and in everyday life. It includes teachers' silencing, correcting, and policing students when they communicate in BL. It is the belief that there is something inherently wrong with BL; therefore, it should be eradicated. It is denying Black students the right to use their native language as a linguistic resource during their language and literacy learning. It is requiring that Black students reject their language and culture to acquire white mainstream English (WME), and it is also insisting that Black students code-switch to avoid discrimination. (p. 9)

Linguistic violence happens in schools that evaluate students according to one monolinguistic yardstick—their use of what has variously been called academic English, standard American English (SAE) (Smith, 2020), white mainstream English (WME) (Baker-Bell, 2020), or dominant academic English (DAE) (Kinloch et al., 2020). Most English and language arts curricula are geared toward students' acquisition of WME, with the claim that it is necessary to learn this form in order to successfully navigate school and life. This continued insistence on gaining mastery of WME privileges and maintains white hegemony. There are few discussions in schools about the linguistic racism that underlies such an insistence. One outcome of judging students according to their use of WME, or suppressing their language in the classroom, is the possibility that they will begin to think about their language, and themselves, as inferior (Baker-Bell, 2020).

In addition to defending students' use of their home language in school, we also need to study the linguistic and historical roots of BL because misunderstandings about it are pervasive. For instance, linguists identify the use of "be" in BL to signal an ongoing or habitual action (e.g., "He be goin to the house Saturday" means "He not only goes to the house this Saturday, but every Saturday") (Charity Hudley & Mallinson, 2010). When we ask our teacher candidates to describe the language patterns of the Black students they teach in Philadelphia classrooms, some describe them with terms like "improper," "ungrammatical," and "slang." These descriptions not only reflect deficit orientations toward the language, they miss the mark about language in general. *Grammatical* simply means that a language is governed by a set of rules that are consistently followed by speakers within particular cultural communities. Investigating the history of BL and its features, such as copula zero ("We cool") and possessives ("John house") (Charity Hudley & Mallinson, 2010), showcases just how grammatically consistent BL is. *All languages are grammatical.* The use of the word *slang* to describe BL also reflects a major misunderstanding about language. Slang generally refers to words, often invented and used by youth, that are here today and gone tomorrow. For example, the word *jawn* is slang used cross-racially to denote "a thing" in Philadelphia. *Go get that jawn!*

In exploring different varieties of English, it is important to recognize that language use is complicated and contextual. Speakers and writers move in and out of local and dominant languages routinely, calling into question the notion of fixed language varieties. Speakers are constantly drawing from a wide repertoire of linguistic resources to negotiate different identities across contexts, within the same context, or even during specific interactions (Alim, 2016). For example, Delicia Tiera Greene (2021) writes about how Black girls blend WME and BL to assert both dominant and local identities while writing journal entries and narratives. Greene's descriptions of *code-meshing* show the fluidity of girls' racial identification through their use of language. In other words, language can have *transracial* effects in that speakers can translate themselves racially and can be translated racially by others through their varied use of language (Alim, 2016). We should think about language not as something that we *have* but something that we *do.* We communicate what we know, think, and want, as well as who we are. *We do language in order to become.*

Scholars in the field of *raciolinguistics* study the ways that language, race, power, and identity are linked. Raciolinguistics is focused on the role that language plays in creating, maintaining, and transforming racial and ethnic identities, challenging the notion that racial identities are fixed (Alim, 2016). Race and language have been historically connected, not only in the United States, but in colonized lands beyond our borders (Flores & Rosa, 2015). Those who speak languages other than English or variations of so-called "standard English" are racialized by the white European conception that WME forms are inherently superior modes of communication. This is an ideological construction—an idea made up by people invested in maintaining language hierarchies and the supremacy of English. By exposing the linkages between race, language, and power, educators can challenge linguistic racism and dismantle the very foundation of white supremacy.

The idea of a standardized English American language has been sustained through white European domination since the colonial period (Rosa & Flores, 2017). Do you recall, as explained in Chapter 4, how concepts of race evolved to promote the interests of white European colonists and their descendants? As Indigenous people and enslaved Africans were regarded as inferior by European colonizers, so were their languages considered incapable of expressing complex thought. This line of thinking continues today, as expressed by linguists Jonathan Rosa and Nelson Flores (2017):

> The raciolinguistic ideologies that organized these colonial relations continue to shape the world order in the postcolonial era by framing racialized subjects' language practices as inadequate for the complex thinking processes needed to navigate the global economy, as well as the targets of anxieties about authenticity and purity. (p. 627)

Raciolinguistics, then, focuses on the reciprocal relationship between race and language as a way to expose continued forms of white supremacy in oral and written communication. A raciolinguistics perspective calls into question the uncritical acceptance of code-switching, which asks students to accept and learn the dominant language code or else. Haven't you heard the warning cries about kids needing to learn SAE in order to do well in school, on standardized tests, in job interviews, and in life? Have you ever questioned whether such promises actually deliver? A raciolinguistic perspective holds that even if speakers of color learn and use SAE or WME, they may be considered "exceptional" in relation to other racialized speakers (Rosa & Flores, 2017), and further, they still may be regarded as inferior by "white listening subjects" (Ahmed, 2012). Having students acquire WME does nothing to challenge white supremacy. Rather, the uncritical insistence that kids learn to code-switch sustains linguistic hierarchies and therefore linguistic violence towards students of color.

Raciolinguistics also examines why students of color continue to be denigrated for their language use while many white speakers of non-standardized English varieties are not subjected to such linguistic policing. Charity Hudley and Mallinson (2010) discuss some of the parallels between southern and Black English patterns in the United States that include various uses of "ain't" and double negatives. While both patterns are identified as "non-standardized forms," linguistic condemnation is mostly directed at and more negatively consequential for BL speakers. The language stigmatization that is experienced by poor and working-class white folks "rarely calls into question their fundamental humanity, serves as grounds for their deportation, or is mobilized as a justification for their extra-judicial killing" (Flores & Rosa, 2015, p. 638). When we ask some of our white-affiliating teacher candidates to describe their communication with family members and friends, they acknowledge using expressions like "Yo, youz guys." They do not consider themselves or others incompetent for using these non-SAE/WME language forms. This is an example of *white linguistic hegemony*—the idea that whiteness, by default, is associated with dominant linguistic forms like WME. White linguistic hegemony insulates white students from the kinds of linguistic racism and denigration that BL students, and students of color who speak varied Englishes, experience continually.

Teachers who are sensitized to how linguistic racism operates in schools are working to dismantle such linguistic denigration in literacy classrooms by inviting students to use a range of Englishes in the classroom (Johnson & Sullivan, 2020). Teachers can honor students' linguistic agility by inviting its use in formal, creative, and technology-based projects and assignments.

MULTILINGUALISM, DYNAMIC BILINGUALISM, AND TRANSLANGUAGING

There are many people in the Philadelphia area who use languages other than English in their homes, and many who are developing their English language capacities. Outside of English, Spanish is the second most used language in the city and is spoken by members of Puerto Rican, Mexican, Dominican, Cuban, and Guatemalan communities, among others. A number of newcomers to Philadelphia bring Vietnamese, Chinese, and Korean linguistic traditions to schools. In addition, there have been a number of Arabic-speaking students entering schools in the Philadelphia region within the last decade. The languages used within communities bind people together and are a central part of identifying with particular cultural groups.

While multilingual speakers are often negatively viewed in schools for the English they lack, they are more cognitively advantaged and prepared for the future compared to monolingual English speakers. Multilingualism is linked to higher cognitive functioning (August & Hakuta, 1997) and the ability to think about the similarities and differences between two or more languages (Bailystok, 2007). Multilingual speakers can draw from a wider range of linguistic resources than monolingual speakers can, and typically think and communicate in more than just one language. Multilingual youth are often expected to translate for their caregivers and elders, so their language dexterity is valued and rewarded in their language communities. Such language proficiency should be valued in schools, but unfortunately these language assets are rarely recognized and celebrated in the United States (García & Kleifgen, 2018). Reflecting on her journey to learn Spanish, Kaitlin shares:

> As a white child growing up in the Philadelphia suburbs in a monolingual household, I wasn't seriously exposed to, nor did I have the option to learn, a second language until high school. Trying to pick up Spanish so late, it took me years, including time spent living abroad, to become proficient. In reflecting on my journey to second-language acquisition, I feel like the fact that we as a nation don't expose our children to regular and sustained second-language learning, like the rest of the world, does us all a disservice. Having taught in schools with different programs, such as bilingual and English immersion, it

> is incredibly frustrating to watch students being robbed of the opportunity to become bilingual when they attend schools with restrictive programming.

Schools with English-only policies and "sink or swim" immersion programs are the most restrictive for multilingual speakers. The goal in these schools is to eliminate students' home language and replace it with English, a *subtractive approach* to language education. Not only are students' cultural identities compromised in these schools, but students' fullest language repertoire is not being utilized and developed. Multilingual speakers "are kept at the basic-language-skill learning level before they are exposed to any books, learn grade-level content, or write for self-expression and presentation of learning" (Fu et al., 2019, p. 10). Further, the demands of the Common Core State Standards mean that multilingual students are "increasingly expected to take and pass high-stakes tests in English as early as a year after their arrival in the United States" (Fu et al., 2019, p. 21). Standardized tests written in English conflate students' understanding of content with their mastery of English and therefore keep students' actual competencies and potential hidden, relegating them to low-level skills-based programs (García & Kleifgen, 2018). These restrictive environments are part of why many multilingual students in U.S. classrooms struggle academically, with only about one quarter of those in New York and California meeting grade-level expectations in 4th grade, and even fewer in 8th grade (Plough & Garcia, 2015). Nationally, around 40% of students identified as English learners will not graduate from high school in 4 years (U.S. Department of Education, n.d.). It is no wonder why many multilingual students leave school prior to graduation (García & Kleifgen, 2018).

Ofelia García (2009) introduced the concept of *dynamic bilingualism* as a way to recognize the wide range of linguistic tools that multilingual students have at their disposal, and that these tools should be used flexibly and in relation to the needs of speakers in particular contexts. García describes dynamic bilingualism as an approach that

> allows the simultaneous coexistence of different languages in communication, accepts translanguaging, and supports the development of multiple linguistic identities to keep a linguistic ecology for efficiency, equity and integration, and responding to both local and global contexts. (p. 119)

Translanguaging is a pedagogical approach that invites students to use their home language in a variety of ways for a variety of learning goals (García & Kleifgen, 2018). Translanguaging occurs when students simultaneously use their "linguistic tools, knowledge, and features from all their languages" (p. 6) to serve their communication needs (Fu et al., 2019). In addition, a translanguaging pedagogy recognizes that multilingual speakers are drawing from a single linguistic system, or repertoire, that contains mixed languages and ways of thinking about language.

In a translanguaging classroom, students might be invited to read texts in the language that is most accessible to them while talking informally in peer groups to prepare for a book discussion. They may take notes in their choice of language as the teacher explains a concept in English. Or, they might be invited to brainstorm with the teacher using one or more languages. They might be given access to reading materials and videos in their most comfortable language. They could also use electronic translation programs to read and write in languages that are most accessible to them. The main point here is that their language is not stopped at the classroom door. Instead, it is utilized to accomplish learning goals.

Translanguaging is not just a pedagogical approach; it is a political stance. "In such a classroom, though the lesson would still have language-specific objectives expecting students to use English in performing certain tasks, it would also include several general linguistic performance objectives that would leverage all their languages" (Fu et al., 2019, p. 27). By encouraging students to draw from their fullest linguistic repertoire, teachers are communicating that English is not superior to other languages. In other words, translanguaging is a way to resist racial hierarchies about languages developed in the context of European (white) colonialism. By affirming students' home language practices, teachers are simultaneously dismantling language hierarchies and inequitable notions of what are appropriate or superior language forms.

Pause and Reflect

1. Think about the language communities near you. How do the speakers in these communities identify racially, culturally, and linguistically?
2. In the schools you know best, describe educators' stances toward students who speak varied Englishes and languages other than English. Would you describe them as welcoming, judgmental, or something else?

CONCLUSION

In this chapter, we have invited you to deconstruct fixed and hierarchical notions of literacy and language. All literacies and languages are legitimate and purposeful ways of communicating. They are dynamic, living practices that are constituted by culture, politics, and history. Our job as educators is to help students understand that no one language form is inherently superior to another. All languages are grammatical—in that they are governed by rules. We educators need to recognize, validate, and honor all of the linguistic forms that students bring to school. We also need to create spaces and opportunities for students to use their most accessible languages to learn (Vygotsky, 1978). They must be able to speak easily and comfortably with each other and their teachers without fear that their language will be denigrated. Correcting a student's speech is silencing. The consequences of correcting students' ways of talking go far beyond missed learning opportunities. A humiliated student will learn to distrust you and will choose not to learn in school as a form of protest, and may even disengage with school entirely (Delpit & Dowdy, 2008). You can turn this around by resisting the linguistic violence that is deeply embedded in schooling systems and by welcoming and recognizing students' diverse, beautiful, and versatile ways of communicating.

Recommended Books

- *Linguistic Justice: Black Language, Literacy, Identity, and Pedagogy* (Baker-Bell, 2020)
- *Understanding English Language Variation in U.S. Schools* (Charity Hudley & Mallinson, 2010)
- *The Skin That We Speak: Thoughts on Language and Culture in the Classroom* (Delpit & Dowdy, 2008)
- *Educating Emergent Bilinguals: Policies, Programs, and Practices for English Language Learners* (García & Kleifgen, 2018)
- *Black Immigrant Literacies: Intersections of Race, Language, and Culture in the Classroom* (Smith & Nero, 2023)
- *Raciolinguistics: How Language Shapes Our Ideas About Race* (Alim, Rickford, & Ball (2016)

CHAPTER 6

Toward Culturally Centered Teaching

> Every child is a dream and their languages are part of who they are. We teachers have the responsibility of being *dreamkeepers*.
>
> —Gloria Ladson-Billings (2009)

How do literacy teachers work as *dreamkeepers* for all children? We know that highly effective literacy teachers provide explicit literacy instruction, engage in constructive exchanges with students, create supportive literacy-rich classrooms, weave reading and writing throughout the curriculum, integrate content-area themes into literacy events, focus on individual needs in small-group settings, have excellent organization and management skills, and develop strong connections with students and their caregivers (Morrow et al., 2009; Wharton-McDonald et al., 1997). Being a dreamkeeper, however, requires something more. Gloria Ladson-Billings (2009) used this word to describe successful teachers of African American students who brought pedagogical expertise *and* sociocultural–political–historical awareness to their work. They possessed a moral stance about students and themselves that translated into student advocacy.

In this chapter, we introduce you to two teachers, Cecilia and Andrea, who demonstrate dreamkeeper-like, advocacy dispositions through their words and actions. Both graduated from our program just recently, but have been teaching in schools with primarily Black-identifying students for a number of years. They developed understandings about equity through the courses we taught, but our program was only one touchpoint in time. Each teacher entered the program with a unique backstory and then continued to develop their advocacy roles through countless moments spent with students, families, colleagues, books, and social media. We consider their stories as snapshots of their most recent thoughts and actions.

Cecilia and Andrea have been teaching in the Philadelphia school district for more than a decade, in highly segregated, primarily Black and Brown communities. As you read about their work, take note of how these teachers 1) see students' knowledge traditions, languages, and literacies as strengths to build on, 2) consider students' identities and life experiences to inform their instruction, and 3) advocate for students by creating classroom environments and curricula that fit with students' life experiences, despite the curriculum restrictions placed upon them. Both are doing this work in schools that emphasize standardized curricula and testing. Later on in the chapter, we will discuss how their work aligns to established teaching frameworks and concepts that support educational equity, including culturally responsive and sustaining teaching (Ladson-Billings, 1995; Paris & Alim, 2014), historically responsive literacy (Muhammad, 2020), funds of knowledge and community wealth (Moll et al., 1992; Yosso, 2005), and critical caring (Valenzuela, 2016; Whipp, 2014).

MEET CECILIA

Orientation

Walking into Cecilia's 5th-grade classroom is like walking into a historical library and museum. Books line an entire 30-foot wall from floor to ceiling, and along the top row is a display of picture books featuring famous people of color. She has amassed this extensive collection over the last 15 years while teaching in Philadelphia's public school district. These books are among the many tools she uses to teach language arts and social studies.

What you don't see in Cecilia's classroom are sticker charts, clips that move up and down on a continuum, or any reference to a behavior management system. Cecilia doesn't have a behavior management system because she does not need one. Instead, she invests in daily community building and she holds restorative meetings on Mondays and Fridays. When she sees a behavior or senses something is brewing, she stops and addresses what is happening in the moment, then moves on. On Mondays and Fridays, her students have a safe space to be heard and to express their thoughts and feelings.

Cecilia took us back to a tender moment during circle time when one of her students, Darius, admitted that he felt *lower than low.* His father had just left his home and he blamed himself. She recalled him saying: *I feel like a piece of garbage.* By then Cecilia had created such a tight community in the classroom that she felt comfortable enough to go around the circle and have each student tell Darius something good about him. Cecilia recalled: *He was so overwhelmed by his classmates' love and support that he began to cry.* She clarified: *This can only happen once you've established trust in the classroom—once you've established a community. The most important thing is that you establish this. You must let them know they are loved.* This process doesn't happen overnight, but Cecilia maintains that consistency, safety, and love are key *soft skills* that teachers need to bring to classrooms, and they need to pass these along to students.

Cecilia is invested in making sure her students *feel like they fit in.* As a biracial-identifying person, Cecilia recalls feelings of displacement as a child attending Philadelphia's schools. At the time of this writing, most of her students affiliated as Black, and she also served a growing population of Spanish-speaking students and recent arrivals from countries in West Africa. All who entered her class were greeted with a sign that said: *All Welcome—All Sizes—All Colors—All Cultures—All Genders.* As a seasoned teacher in the building, other teachers flocked to her classroom after school to have a Coke, shoot the breeze, and debrief about the day. It is clear that other teachers have looked to her for guidance and mentoring.

Prior to entering our reading-specialist master's degree program, Cecilia was a practicing attorney and legal advocate. Her life experiences, her teaching experience, and her law background have made her a fierce advocate for her students. She proudly refers to her students as "scholars," reflecting that she sees and treats them as intellectuals. She has seen a revolving door of leadership in her current school and so for her students, and their families, she maintained a constant and steady presence. She has kept up with topics related to culturally sustaining pedagogy, closely following the work of scholars like Bettina Love and Gholdy Muhammad.

Curriculum and Teaching

As the designated language arts/social studies teacher for the 5th grade, Cecilia was asked to use a curriculum called *Wit and Wisdom* to guide her teaching in both subject areas. It includes original literature selections that serve as "mirrors, windows, and sliding glass doors" (Bishop, 1990) and videos that provide additional historical context for the literature. The curriculum includes historical fiction that addresses issues of racial injustice. Cecilia used these stories to build students' essay-writing skills. For instance, the 5th-grade anthology includes the book *Thunder Rolling in the Mountains* (O'Dell, 1992) about how the U.S. government drove the Nez Perce Indians off their land in the late 1800s. Cecilia lit up recalling how her students *really got into this story.* To prepare students to write critical essays about this story, she modeled ways to take evidence from the book. The students' task was to explain why the Nez Perce homeland was important to both groups, based on their different cultural beliefs and values. The completed essays not only reflected students' ability to use text evidence to show both groups' cultural positionings, but many students used this assignment to defend the rights of the Nez Perce. One student began her essay with a clear position: *How would you feel if someone wanted your home?* She then proceeded to detail how the government was motivated by gold and appeasing the settlers, while the Nez Perce were invested in keeping the only homeland they had known for thousands of years. Cecilia observed: *They really became empathetic to the plight of Native people through writing about this story.*

Cecilia also used other literature selections to teach writing while sustaining students' identities and linking with students' families. For instance, she used the *My Name* chapter in *The House on Mango Street* (Cisneros, 1984) to guide students' writing about their names because, as she stated, *how your name is treated by teachers at school is important.* Cecilia liked using this vignette because it included craft features such as descriptive language and telling a story within a story, which she invited her students to try. She also used this literature as a springboard to ask family members about the origins of their names: *I had them analyze Cisneros's narrative, then go home and interview their caregivers about their names.* Students were invited to use whatever language they felt most comfortable using to write their own stories about their names: *They could use Spanish, Arabic, . . . any language they want.* Cecilia affirms her students' language, which includes their use of Black Language. In Cecilia's classroom the *mother tongue,* as she refers to it, is recognized and celebrated, it is not discounted or denigrated.

While Cecilia has been able to maximize her use of *Wit and Wisdom* to teach elements of essay writing, she expressed frustration at not being able to do more narrative writing with her students, especially her boy scholars who she thought sometimes struggled to express themselves. Being the advocate she is, she devised a plan to establish an after-school writer's club for boys: *You can get profound stuff when you are dealing with just the boys.* In this club, she planned to include mini-lessons, discussions, sharing, and peer conferencing. She said: *I could go deeper, and they will be able to express themselves and be heard, just for themselves, not for a grade.*

Cecilia designed her social studies curriculum from scratch, bringing her expertise of the American Revolution to the task, along with an abundance of resources from Philadelphia's many historical organizations. For example, she regularly used *History Hunters* (https://www.historyhunters.org), a literacy-based educational program centered in Philadelphia's Germantown, a community that is rich in historical sites. Through the program, her students could act as investigative reporters while visiting sites such as the Johnson House, an early abolitionist home that served as a way station along the Underground Railroad. Adding to her American history curriculum, Cecilia highlighted the life and accomplishments of James Forten, a Philadelphia sailmaker and businessman who used his fortune to abolish slavery and obtain civil rights for Black citizens.

Cecilia is adamant about reconceptualizing the social studies curriculum to sustain students' positive identities. In most schools' curricula, Black history begins in 1619 with the importation of enslaved Africans to Jamestown. Cecilia found this to be an unacceptable curricular structure, and so she rearranged the curriculum to emphasize Black joy and a heritage of brilliance.

> The first time my Black and Brown children see themselves reflected in history is when they learn about the importation of enslaved people to Jamestown in 1619. I would hate to think that the curriculum I teach may contribute to a child seeing their racial identity in a negative light. Slavery is an important part of the American story. It should be taught. But it should not be the initial image that students see of themselves in history. So I choose to veer from the required curriculum and first teach my students the history of Black joy. We study the kingdoms, inventions, and the brilliance of ancient African kingdoms as an introduction to history.

Caregivers and Community

Cecilia routinely alters other parts of her curricula to make her classroom walls permeable to the surrounding community and to engage students in literacy and learning practices that align with their interests. As a leader and mentor, Cecilia also challenged her colleagues to reframe deficit narratives around caregiver engagement. She recalled a time when her school had issued several invitations to caregivers, including via social media, to attend a school advisory meeting, but few showed up. Low caregiver attendance at this event only exacerbated her colleagues' deficit views of them. Cecilia reasoned that there needed to be a *seismic shift at my school in the way we perceive families*. She explained:

> Viewing families as "experts" of their children who can positively contribute to their education would be a good start. We could demonstrate this by building personal relationships with parents through things like "good news" phone calls, attending student events outside of school, and soliciting parents to come share their expertise with students. Our Back to School Night at the beginning of the year is generally well attended. Using that as an opportunity to connect with parents, having a conversation with them and their child rather than talking at them, could ease parental anxiety. At Back-to-School Night I purposely push all the desks to one side of the room and put all chairs in a circle and sit alongside my parents. It puts us more on equal footing. Culturally relevant teaching, and invitations for parents to just not visit, but share and teach in the classroom would go a long way to help families realize that the school values the unique voice that their experiences afford them.

Cecilia's approach to caregivers is one of respect. Seeing caregivers as experts of their children, rearranging her classroom to sit alongside caregivers at Back to School Night, and inviting caregivers to be teachers in her classroom during the school year are all ways that Cecilia connected with families to build a strong foundation for learning in her classroom. We will hear more from Cecilia in Chapter 7.

MEET ANDREA

Orientation

If you're walking into Andrea's classroom, well . . . you'll be in good company. Andrea, and her room, have a way of drawing students in. Andrea's bright, airy, bubbly disposition translates closely into her physical space. Her infectious laugh can be heard from far down the hallway. In her cozy, comfortable room, desks are arranged in small groups, while books representing diverse genres, authors, and subjects line the shelves. She has grown famous in her building for having quite an array of graphic novels, which bring many inquiring minds to her door. It's clear from students' demeanors, interactions, and giggles, that this is a safe and welcoming space.

Andrea is a white, monolingual teacher of 4th-graders who refers to her students as "scholars." While she does not identify racially with her students, she has amassed several layers of connection with them as a decade-plus veteran of the Philadelphia school district. She attends community/neighborhood events and prioritizes opportunities for small talk with caregivers during drop-off and pickup from school. As a parent raising young school-age children and as the spouse of a partner who is frequently away for work, she feels connected to most of her students' caregivers, who are also challenged with juggling job and childcare responsibilities.

Andrea taught in a few different district schools before landing in one that serves almost exclusively African American students. The community has been plagued by gun violence over the last few years. During the pandemic, the city experienced a surge in teenage homicides, often precipitated by drug-related turf wars and instances of retaliation (Johanson, 2020). Andrea's students have witnessed shootings while in the schoolyard and her school is regularly forced to lock down as a safety precaution. She has witnessed an increase in students' trauma in response to the uptick in neighborhood violence.

Andrea feels pressure from all around—from the school district, her administration, and even herself, to "pick up where she left off" after lockdowns and engage students in academics each minute of the day. She has come to believe, however, that learning cannot happen when students are anxious or upset or when, as she says, *the light has left their eyes*. She notes: *They're not having it, they're not hearing anything,* and *they're not connecting to anything*. She has used a number of strategies to soothe and calm her students so they can reengage in learning. One strategy that she has used successfully with individual students who are very upset involves squeezing their hands, as she explains:

> It's me just squeezing their hand and saying, "Squeeze back when you're ready. Squeeze when you're back with me, and you're ready to move forward." And sure, sometimes they'd be so angry or so upset and it would take a long time. But it's something small that I could do, and still monitor the class, still kind of keep my other students going, but also give that student the attention they needed and let them know that I was there and they were there. It was just getting them to an okay space, a place where they could kind of bring themselves back to a comfortable emotional state using a sensory practice.

Another strategy Andrea uses when her students are overstimulated is to have them take a momentary "reset" break:

> We, all, everyone, every student, and even me, would put our heads down and take a minute. I would set a timer, and I'd be like, "Okay, let's do one minute of calm," and literally every time that it was broken, we just restarted it. It was like, "Oh, it's okay. We're going to restart."

Andrea emphasizes that these strategies are not framed as punishments, but rather, as loving and positive approaches for helping students get back on track so they can bring their best selves to learning. She believes these approaches are far more responsive to students' emotional states than the coaching conversations that the administration wants her to do, a school reform model adapted from the work of Gross Cheliotes and Reilly (2010) by which teachers "coach" their students in intentional ways to promote growth and change. Andrea believes these staged coaching conversations do not help students because they do not acknowledge what students are experiencing at the moment. What they need, she believes, is a teacher who sees and acknowledges their feelings at the very time they are experiencing them.

Along with responding to students' social and emotional needs, Andrea has been attentive to creating a positive classroom community with her students. This year she decided to give in to her students' requests to watch *Coco Melon*—a cartoon program for youngsters that features nursery rhymes and songs. Andrea resisted at first because she felt it was not the best use of her 4th-graders' school time. She discovered, however, that allowing her students to watch it for a few minutes after lunch helped them bond, creating an emotionally supportive, family-like atmosphere that Andrea felt her students needed: *I have videos of them literally sitting as a group, just singing together. They've never been more connected as a team and as a group than when they were watching* Coco Melon. *They needed this.*

By paying close attention to what her students need, Andrea establishes a welcoming and joyful learning environment for them. She also draws from her students' interests to make her classroom culturally centered. For example, Andrea knew that her students loved singer–songwriter Cardi B, who was recently named the "Reigning Queen of Hip Hop" (Saint-Louis, 2023). She decorated her classroom walls with inspiring quotations, like "Knock me down 9 times, but I get up 10." When one of her colleagues criticized Andrea for using Cardi B's words in her classroom, Andrea defended her decision:

> A peer came to be and said, "You should not have that up there. That person is so sexualized. You're telling our students they should be that way." And I was like, "Well, I'm not telling them how to be. Either way. This is somebody that is a role model for them, whether we agree with it or not. This is someone that they look up to. This is the person that they are hearing from. AND, by the way, this is a great quote. This is a quote that they could learn from, and they should learn from, and that they can be inspired by." So the quotes stayed.

By insisting that Cardi B's words remain on her classroom walls, Andrea drew a proverbial line in the sand and stood with her students. She recognized the significance of the artist's message as positive and inspiring, and she conveyed this message to her disgruntled colleague, who Andrea felt "did not get it." Eventually they settled on agreeing to disagree.

Curriculum and Teaching

Like Cecilia, Andrea is one of the more senior teachers in her building, and feels she has the confidence and authority to make decisions to change or augment the curriculum to suit the needs of her students.

> I don't think I've ever gotten pushback from a supervisor as far as what I do in my classroom and any liberties I may take with the curriculum. I'm somebody who does their job and I'm pretty confident in myself, and my decision-making, especially when it's in the best interest of my students, so I think that confidence usually translates well.

Andrea is conscious about having her students identify with school reading materials, but found that her literacy curriculum lacked books that would resonate with their day-to-day experiences. She did not feel tethered to using the district's reading list, and so brought in books like *One Crazy Summer* (Williams-Garcia, 2011) with strong and memorable African American characters. She used this book to meet curriculum standards for 4th grade, which included analysis of plot, characters, theme, and the examination of the features of realistic historical fiction. Andrea also used *One Crazy Summer* to teach writing; she used it to show students how the author authenticates story characters through their language. Here, she explains how and why she used the book as a mentor text to help students craft their own narratives using dialogue:

> In the book, AAVE is written into the dialogue and it's important for my students to see that. We talk about how this is when somebody's speaking in the book versus when the author is narrating. We talk about how the use of AAVE makes sense in the book when the characters are engaged in dialogue because this is how people talk. I encourage my students to practice that in their own writing, especially when they're going to tell a story.

Andrea saw her students' languages through a capacity lens and invited them to use their home language in the classroom. She frequently says: *Whatever language you are most comfortable using, use it.* She reminds students to focus on making sure they write so that their audience can understand the message: *Understanding their audience is an important life skill and I'll say, "In anything that you're doing, it's important to understand your audience."*

Andrea also fosters students' sense of audience through text-dependent analysis (TDA) assignments. TDAs, tied to the state's literacy test, require that students draw evidence from literary or informational texts to write short essays. Andrea uses the TDA as a springboard to teach students about writing for different audiences. She models audience awareness by giving examples of how she talks to her friends versus how she talks to her children versus how she talks to the school principal. She invites students to do the same through simulation activities where they take otherwise-related topics and discuss them in small informal groups. Then, Andrea asks students to collaborate in groups to draft a more formal presentation on the topic for an unknown audience. After students adjust their writing to fit the audience, they analyze the linguistic differences between the informal language they used initially and the formal language they used in the written draft. Andrea has observed her students' high engagement with this literacy event because they begin with what is most familiar to them—their language—and then get to work collaboratively in the writing and reflection parts of the activity.

While Andrea does not currently have emergent bilinguals in her classroom, she has in the past and expects that she will again. In her graduate program, she learned about the subtractive nature of schooling for emergent bilinguals and began to scrutinize this trend in the district. Reading and talking about the book *Educating Emergent Bilinguals* (García & Kleifgen, 2018) provided an important lens through which to identify language inequities in the district:

> The bilingual programs I have observed have either been subtractive or nonexistent. The most common program I have seen is an immersion system in a general education classroom with a pull-out English learning support class. In

> this program, the students' home languages were not considered, valued, or reinforced as the students attempted to learn English in a high-pressure situation.

Earlier in her career, while teaching in another school, she recalled a pair of Spanish-speaking sisters who entered school with little knowledge of English. The girls sat together in the back of the classroom their entire first year, being mostly ignored for much of the day, except when they were pulled out for small-group English instruction. In the course of 3 years, Andrea noticed the sisters' growing ability to use conversational English. They still, however, struggled academically. Andrea lamented that much more could have been done to welcome these girls' language in order to help them learn:

> The home language of Spanish could have been reinforced while making connections to the English language as they began to fold in their understanding of the new language. In this method, the theoretical ideas of linguistic interdependence and common underlying proficiency were not utilized to support the holistic education of these students. There are many commonalities between English and Spanish that would have helped these two students—and countless others—become bilingual, versus focusing on English-only instruction at the expense of their home language.

Andrea has not forgotten these sisters and often wonders what happened to them as they were passed through the system. She vows that when emergent bilinguals come to her classroom as she expects they will, she will recognize and tap into their linguistic gifts.

Let's stop now to reflect on the ways these teachers supported, cared for, and taught their students.

PAUSE AND REFLECT:

1. What elements of Cecilia's and Andrea's beliefs and teaching practices stood out to you?
2. What elements of their practice can you envision for yourself?

EXAMINING TEACHERS AND TEACHING THROUGH ADVOCACY-FOCUSED FRAMEWORKS

Cecilia and Andrea are teachers whose words and deeds exemplify those found in several equity-focused teaching frameworks. In this section, we will highlight many of the central ideas of these frameworks. Later, we will return to the teachers to connect their stances and actions to various ideas in the frameworks. We will also point out the ways they go beyond these frameworks to advocate for their students in specific ways.

Culturally Relevant/Sustaining Teaching

Recall our discussion at the start of this chapter about *dreamkeepers,* a term used by Gloria Ladson-Billings to describe eight highly successful teachers of African American students. Ladson-Billings conceptualized these teachers' practices as culturally relevant, spawning a movement that has penetrated many schools of education and the language of many teachers. Cultural relevance focuses on producing students who can achieve academically, demonstrate cultural competence, and "understand and critique the existing social order" (p. 474). Ladson-Billings urged educators to demand students' academic excellence by maintaining high expectations, recognizing their assets, and inspiring them to see academic achievement as part of their cultural legacy. She envisioned classrooms where students' cultural competence could be maintained through a variety of means, including using cultural references to teach new concepts, welcoming parents or community members into classrooms to share their expertise, and encouraging students to express themselves in their home languages. Further, she indicated that developing students' sociopolitical consciousness would help prepare them to question and work against structures and institutions that produce and maintain social inequities.

As discussed in Chapter 1, Django Paris introduced the term *culturally sustaining* teaching when he questioned whether terms like *responsive* or *relevant* "go far enough in their orientation to the languages and literacies and other cultural practices of communities marginalized by systemic inequalities to ensure the valuing and maintenance of our multiethnic and multilingual society (Paris, 2012, p. 93). Paris argued "it is quite possible to be relevant to something or responsive to it without ensuring its continuing presence in a student's *repertoires of practice* (Gutiérrez & Rogoff, 2003), and so its presence in our classrooms and communities" (p. 95). Culturally sustaining pedagogy (CSP) guides educators to create classrooms and learning experiences that *center* students' linguistic and cultural knowledge.

Paris urged educators to consider how cultural practices of students and communities are continuously shifting. Youth communities embrace traditional cultural practices while continuing to add to and change these practices. Paris warned educators not to essentialize or be "overly deterministic in our linkages of language and other cultural practices to certain racial and ethnic groups in approaching what it is we are seeking to sustain" (2012, p. 95). For example, he discusses the ways African American youth navigate identities through Black Language and hip-hop cultures while those who identify as Latinx may appropriate these cultural modes in addition to those connected with Caribbean American cultures. What is considered "cultural practice" is constantly in flux, requiring that educators become students of the youth cultures they serve.

Historically Responsive Teaching

Closely related to CSP is *historically responsive literacy* (HRL), conceptualized by Gholdy Muhammad (2020) and described in her book *Cultivating Genius: An Equity Framework for Culturally and Historically Responsive Literacy*. Muhammad's framework is rooted in the literary societies of the 1800s, in which Black citizens met regularly to "construct knowledge and engage one another toward cultivating a literary culture" (p. 8). Literacy society members understood the transformative power of literacy to improve self and society, and used their literacy knowledge to confront racism. Muhammad argues for a reconceptualization of literacy education that mirrors the goals and experiences of these society members to focus on building students' identities, skills, intellect, and critical abilities. She explains:

> Each time early Black readers came together to read, write, think, and learn, they were making sense of who they were (identity), developing their proficiencies in the content they were learning within (skills), becoming smarter about something or gaining new knowledge and concepts in the world (intellect), and finally, developing the ability to read texts (including print text and social contexts) to understand power, authority and anti-oppression (criticality). (p. 12)

Muhammad's notion of criticality mirrors perspectives on critical literacy and critical pedagogy that are discussed in the next chapter. HRL takes a multiple literacies and languages perspective. It encourages educators to move beyond normative classroom literacy practices and adopt a multiliteracies approach that honors the various ways that students of color use spoken and printed language.

Funds of Knowledge/Community Wealth

CRT/CST, and HRL frameworks are based on the concepts of "funds of knowledge" (González et al., 2005) and "community wealth" (Yosso, 2005). Funds of knowledge are "historically accumulated and culturally developed bodies of knowledge and skills essential for household or individual functioning and well-being" (Moll et al., 1992, p. 133). All too often, the knowledge and skills that students construct through their home/community-based social engagements are not legitimized in schools. Propelled by an interest in challenging deficit understandings of working-class families, Moll's research team collaborated with teachers to observe and interview family members primarily within immigrant and U.S.-born Latinx communities in Tucson, Arizona. By learning about the social history of families, their labor experiences, and their social networking activities, Moll and his colleagues categorized the knowledge and resources that different families possessed. Examples of household knowledge include farming, ranching, timbering, infant care, cooking, midwifery, first aid procedures, and house and car maintenance.

In conceptualizing how to utilize families' funds of knowledge in school, a few of the team members learned that a student, Carlos, sold Mexican candy to a neighbor. They also learned that a parent in the community was an expert candy-maker. Teachers working with the research team translated this knowledge into curricula and created a literacy-based candy-making unit that addressed a number of academic concepts, including nutritional value of candy, the use of vegetable dyes and real fruit in Mexican candy versus American candy, and the consumption and production of candy. The teachers invited students' questions, which launched a range of inquiries that addressed math, science, health, consumer education, cross-cultural practices, advertising, and food production. By connecting students' knowledge traditions to specific academic concepts, the team not only legitimized students' experiences, but found their efforts to be highly engaging. At the conclusion of the unit, students formulated many more questions: "From the questions the students came up with alone, we could have continued investigating using innumerable research and critical thinking skills for a considerable part of the year" (p. 139).

Teaching in culturally sustaining ways means knowing about students' communities. It also means recognizing and appreciating the abundance of wealth that exists in every community. In the Community Cultural Wealth Model, Tara Yosso (2005) inventoried several varieties of *capital* within communities of Color, including social, familial, aspirational, navigational, and resistance forms of cultural capital. These forms are highlighted in Table 6.1.

Table 6.1. Forms of Community Cultural Wealth

Capital Type	Description
Social	Networks of people in churches, business, and community organizations that offer young people affirmation, guidance, leadership skills, and opportunities
Familial	The ways that immediate and extended family members support students' well-being and academic goals
Aspirational	Community members' capacity to maintain their hopes and dreams in the face of economic hardships; teachers, school administrators, clergy, small business owners, skilled workers, and others in a community show young children what is possible to attain
Navigational	The ability of community residents to maneuver through social systems that were designed by the dominant mainstream culture, exists and becomes an instrument in students' lives
Resistance	Knowledge and skills fostered through oppositional behavior that challenges inequality (e.g., Freire, 1970, 1973; Giroux, 1983; McLaren, 1994)

Concepts of cultural capital and community wealth fit with *reality pedagogy* that is based on inviting the everyday experiences of youth (Emdin, 2016) in the classroom to honor students' voices, worlds, and literacy practices. One promising area of scholarship looks at how teachers tap youth and community capital through the use of digital tools (blog posts, podcasts, TED talks) (Lewis, 2018; Greene, 2021). These tools allow students to engage in counter-storytelling that directly challenges European/Western (white) narratives that tend to dominate in school.

Caring With Political Clarity

Teachers who *care with political clarity* (Roberts, 2010; Rolon-Dow, 2005; Whipp, 2014) teach in ways that align with CRT/CST and HRL because they are highly conscious of the sociocultural, sociopolitical contexts in which they and their students live. They understand how racist systems of schooling and society work against their students and so they position themselves to challenge and dismantle these systems. They actively seek changes to curriculum, policies, and practices that undermine students' educational outcomes.

Do you recall Laura from Chapter 1? She clearly understood the political and racialized contexts that she and her students occupied. She combined emotional warmth with high academic and behavioral expectations (Irvine, 2003; Siddle Walker, 2001; Valenzuela, 1999), drew from students cultural "funds of knowledge" (Moll et al., 1992) and cultural capital (Yosso, 2005) to teach, viewed caregivers and community members as partners and allies in supporting students (Ladson-Billings, 2009; Rolon-Dow, 2005; Valenzuela, 1999), built students' cultural competence and identities (Ladson-Billings, 1995; Muhammad, 2020; Valenzuela, 1999), maintained a laser-sharp focus on academic achievement and skill-building (Ladson-Billings, 1995; Muhammad, 2020) and advocated for students by seeking changes to curriculum, policies, and practices that undermine students' development (Ladson-Billings, 1995; Nieto, 2005; Rolon-Dow, 2005; Valenzuela, 1999). Warm demanders exemplify a specific type of advocacy-focused teacher, one that not only challenges unjust schooling practices, but who also establishes a *culture of love* in the classroom (Lewis, 2018).

Pause and Reflect

1. What are some ideas that are common across these frameworks and concepts?
2. Name some ways that literacy teachers can draw from students' funds of knowledge to develop students' reading or writing abilities.

SEEING TEACHERS WITHIN AND BEYOND FRAMEWORKS

In reading about teaching frameworks, it is likely that you have already made connections between what the scholarship defines as equity/advocacy-focused teaching and what Cecilia and Andrea say and do. Both teachers recognized the sociocultural, sociopolitical, sociohistorical elements that shaped their students' lives and opportunities, and they drew from students' funds of knowledge and community/cultural wealth to establish loving, community-centered, culturally affirming classrooms. Both teachers rejected subtractive views of literacy and language that delegitimize their students' ways of speaking and writing. Both changed or augmented the curriculum to foster students' cultural identities and their affiliations with school. Cecilia challenged the premise of beginning a U.S. history curriculum with Black enslavement and instead changed it to reflect a history that communicates an ancestral legacy of Black joy and intellectualism. Andrea affirmed her students' identification with school by standing her ground and insisting that artists like Cardi B communicate in ways that resonate with students. Similarly, Andrea responded to a gap in her school's reading materials by importing books like *One Crazy Summer* to teach literacy. As such, both teachers preserve students' identities while advancing their literacy development. Gholdy Muhammad (2020) explains that when 19th-century literacy society members gathered to read, write, think, and learn, they were making sense of who they were; their collaborations were about asserting their literate identities amid many societal challenges.

Neither teacher used a behavior management system. Both teachers teach us to be sensitive to students' social and emotional needs, and to be aware of the ways that trauma undermines students' ability to learn. Andrea acknowledged students' anxieties and fears by providing soothing and calming hand-squeezing exercises. She showed us that establishing a safe and trusting community sometimes means listening to students when they ask to spend a few minutes watching programs that they love, like *Coco Melon*. Her giving in to this request paid dividends in the form of classroom community bonding. Cecilia employed regular restorative meetings that embraced students in circles of love and appreciation. She also positioned caregivers as resources for creating culturally welcoming classrooms and schools. Both teachers' stances and actions resemble those who care with political clarity (Roberts, 2010; Rolon-Dow, 2005; Whipp, 2014).

If we look closely at these teachers' dispositions, we see they have established firm commitments to their students, as a reflection of their dedication to continually learning and adjusting their instruction around the needs of their students. Both continue to make connections between teaching and equity studies. Cecilia reads equity-focused books and articles by scholars such as Bettina Love and Gholdy Muhammad. Andrea fortifies her teaching by watching successful fellow educators, following students' interests and experiences, and finding children's literature that reflects their realities. Each teacher has grown to be a highly respected professional by their school leadership team. They are trusted to make decisions that are in the best interests of their students and have the latitude to enact instruction in ways they see fit. Both are seen as having attained expert competencies within the landscape of practice (Wenger-Trayner & Wenger-Trayner, 2015), and both are committed to learning about students' lives and experiences and connecting this knowledge to literacy practice.

CONCLUSION

When we think about what the scholarship says about what we can do to make literacy learning more equitable for students, and the elements that weigh against our ability to do this work, it is easy to become discouraged. Even so, the Cecilias and Andreas of the profession exist, and they show us what is possible. We want you to see how advocacy work can be possible for *you*. Seeing obstacles as opportunities and problems as possibilities is a charge that we hope spreads like wildfire. In the next chapter, we will explore how teachers raise students' critical consciousness through transacting with literature and using literacy to solve real-world problems.

Recommended Books

- *Cultivating Genius: An Equity Framework for Culturally and Historically Responsive Teaching* (Muhammad, 2020)
- *Culturally Relevant Pedagogy: Asking a Different Question* (Ladson-Billings & Paris, 2021)
- *Culturally Sustaining Language and Literacy Practices for PreK–3: The Children Come Full* (Nash & Arce-Boardman, 2022)
- *Culturally Sustaining Literacy Pedagogies: Honoring Students' Heritages, Literacies, and Languages* (Cantrell, Walker-Dalhouse & Lazar, 2022)

CHAPTER 7

Toward Critical Teaching

> Education is the most powerful weapon which you can use to change the world.
>
> —Nelson Mandela (1990)

In front of an international audience of global leaders in 2018, Greta Thunberg famously declared: "*I have learned you are never too small to make a difference*" (UN Climate Change, 2018). And we concur. Adults are far from being the only agents capable of creating and inspiring change, locally, nationally, and globally. In the United States, youth have a long history of civic and social engagement both inside and outside of schools. Recently, we have seen a surge in activism with students staging mass walk-outs, starting social media campaigns, testifying before Congress, and fun-draising in support of issues like racial inequality, gun control, LGBTQIA+ rights, and climate change. These acts, and the courageous young people who stand behind them, give us great hope for the future. As advocacy-focused educators, it's important to appreciate their work, and support the individuals and groups out there in our communities, schools, and class-rooms living and breathing it.

Activism and literacy go hand in hand. Communicating about social issues involves a range of literate behaviors, yet classroom literacy activities are rarely channeled into activist goals. Instead of learning that literacy involves critical and purposeful communication for the common good, most students learn that literacy is a *skill to be practiced*. In the primary grades students *practice* reading aloud, making inferences, finding main ideas, and writing coherent paragraphs. As adolescents, they *practice* writing five-paragraph essays and lab reports. All this practicing helps students develop literate capacities, but it does little to engage students purposefully and critically in the world around them.

What if students could be directed to make the world a better and more equitable place *through school literacy events? What if students made inferences in order to consider dominant or missing voices in a text? What if they considered whether "main" ideas represent the perspectives of those who are culturally dominant or subjugated? What if they published their writing to educate others about food deserts in their community? What if they wrote lab reports about the quality of the drinking water in schools, and later wrote letters to the school board expressing a need to improve school water quality?* These questions guide us to think about how we can use literacies to learn about and dismantle injustices, and in doing so, make literacy learning not only purposeful, but transformative.

In the first part of this chapter, we will discuss *critical literacy* as a way to help students scrutinize texts to examine injustices that directly impact their lives. In the second part of the chapter, we will explore how the teachers in our local network support their students to solve real-world problems through engaging in *action activism* in their communities.

CRITICAL LITERACY: QUESTIONING TEXTS AND THE WORLD

Critical literacy (CL) focuses on scrutinizing texts in order to become informed citizens who can work for social equity (Darder et al., 2009; Janks, 2018, McLean et al., 2009). CL aligns with Gloria Ladson-Billings's (1995) notion of developing students' *sociopolitical consciousness* "that allows them to critique the cultural norms, values, mores, and institutions that produce and maintain social inequities" (p. 162) to prepare students for active citizenship. It also connects to Gholdy Muhammad's (2020) idea of *criticality,* "the capacity to read, write, and think in the context of understanding power, privilege, and oppression" (p. 12) to understand injustice and work toward social transformation.

CL is linked to *critical pedagogy,* which centers on interrogating various dimensions of schooling, education, and pedagogy for social justice and democratic aims. Several educational philosophers have argued that schools in the United States do not produce intellectuals who can participate in democratic decision-making and the struggle for equality (Giroux, 1987; Lankshear & McLaren, 1993; Macedo, 2000). Henri Giroux (1987) argued that literacy education focuses on preparing people for the workforce and providing them with knowledge based on the history and traditions of the culturally dominant.

Charges that schools produce uncritical graduates who seek to preserve the status quo resonate today when we think about events like January 6, 2021. If generations of school children were educated to question media messages, would they be taken in by President Trump's call to storm the U.S. Capitol to keep him in office? This is a question that no one can really answer, but it gets us thinking about our role in educating students to question texts of all types, including those that seem innocuous. *How can we find ways to create critically informed citizens within schooling systems that are mainly focused on giving students job skills?* In our post-truth world of alternative facts, lies, and bullshit, Hilary Janks (2018) stated that now more than ever, "we need to be wary of those who want to be the master in control of language and meaning" (p. 95). This is why critical literacy is so vitally important to us. This is why we need to be able to read texts critically and help our students do the same.

Critical literacy is based on the premise that no text is neutral. All book authors, illustrators, podcast hosts, video producers, and the like have been shaped to see the world a certain way, and they all communicate particular perspectives through their creations. Whether they are intentional or not, text creators have an agenda—even those who write about something as seemingly neutral as the weather! Critical literacy offers a way to unpack this agenda.

Translated into literacy instruction, teachers can invite students to examine different kinds of texts for messages about what is said and unsaid about social inequality and power dynamics (Cervetti et al., 2001; Comber & Simpson, 2001; Heffernan, 2004; McDaniel, 2006; Stevens & Bean, 2007; Vasquez, 2003, 2004; Wells et al., 2022). Teachers who stress critical literacy invite students to investigate whose voices are represented and whose are excluded in a given text (including books, media, art, and other creations). The idea is to help students become informed about social inequalities so they may ultimately engage in social action campaigns to address these problems (Janks, 2018).

Based on an extensive review of the literature, Lewison et al. (2002) identified four dimensions of critical literacy that continue to guide educators to facilitate critical discussions of texts. They include:

1. Disrupting the commonplace: We disrupt the commonplace when we acknowledge and analyze how texts, including popular culture and media, have shaped our identities and biases.
2. Interrogating multiple viewpoints: When we interrogate multiple viewpoints, we are scrutinizing texts to see whose voices are dominant, whose are missing, and why some voices are silenced while others are heard.
3. Focusing on sociopolitical issues: We focus on sociopolitical issues to identify unequal power relationships, including the ways that some are systemically advantaged while others are disadvantaged.
4. Taking ongoing action to promote social justice: When we take ongoing action to promote social justice, we use literacy to promote social change and support students in their development as social activists.

Engaging and reflecting on these four dimensions of critical literacy allows readers to construct understandings, perspectives, and language to then take action to promote social justice.

Let's consider how one might address these dimensions of critical literacy using the picture book *What I See: Anti-Asian Racism from the Eyes of a Child* (2021) by Christine T. Leung. This book is about the violence directed toward Asians and Pacific Islanders in the wake of the global pandemic. The narrator is a young girl who tells readers about the myths associated with Asian American and Pacific Islander (AAPI) communities, including a new one—that they are responsible for the pandemic. She tells about people wanting to hurt her and those she cares about, even the elders in her community. She recognizes that she must not be silent, and instead, decides to use her voice to confront the hatred she sees. The narrator points out that all of us are beautiful; the world is so big that everyone can fit, and no one is to blame for the pandemic. She states that the way to recover from the pandemic is for all to join together to fight the virus instead of each other.

Table 7.1 shows how a teacher might use this book and the critical literacy framework described by Lewison et al. (2002) to foster a critical discussion about the treatment of people in AAPI communities:

We are not suggesting that all of the questions contained in Table 7.1 be used to facilitate critical dialogues of Leung's book. The table provides *possible* avenues for exploring the stereotypes associated with people in AAPI communities, how they are perpetuated across different types of texts, and how these stereotypes connect with the historical subjugation of people in diverse AAPI communities. The goal for such a discussion is to invite student decision-making and action in order to confront

Table 7.1. Dimensions of Critical Literacy

Dimensions	Questions
Disrupting the commonplace	How does the author portray people in AAPI communities? Are they shown as victims, villains, or community organizers? What tells you this? How are people in AAPI communities typically shown in books or films? What do you think about these portrayals?
Interrogating multiple viewpoints	Whose voices are present in this book? Whose are missing? What does the author tell us about the views of people in AAPI communities? What does the author tell us about the views of people in other racial/ethnic communities?
Focusing on sociopolitical issues	How have people in AAPI communities been treated in this country? How have their rights been denied? How can we explore this?
Taking action to promote social justice	What can we do to call out violence toward people in AAPI communities? How can we do something about the violence that local AAPI communities experience?

stereotyping and stop the violence perpetrated against those in AAPI communities.

When we connect texts to specific experiences within the communities where we live and teach, we make critical literacy even more relevant for students. For instance, we can imagine accompanying Leung's book with a curated text set that includes newspaper accounts from the *Philadelphia Inquirer* about local attacks on members of AAPI communities from 2019 to 2021. We might also use the Wider Horizons for You and Yours (WHYY) series titled *Asian Americans and Pacific Islanders: A Philadelphia Story,* which chronicles the history of AAPI communities in Philadelphia, including a recent solidarity rally and march against violence directed toward these communities. These resources reveal the contributions and cultural wealth of AAPI communities, as well as how they have responded to attacks and systemic subjugation. As such, the curated text set would explore the sociopolitical history and current realities of AAPI members, as reflected in Lewiston et al.'s framework.

Let's see how two teachers from our graduate program network have applied the ideas of critical literacy to their teaching practices. In describing their work, we will refer to particular elements of critical literacy teaching (Lewison et al., 2002) that each teacher emphasizes.

MEET JENNIFER

Jennifer, a Vietnamese American teacher, is one of our recent program graduates who decided she would use literature to disrupt her students' commonplace assumptions about various cultural communities, including her own. In her undergraduate program and her master's-level university-sponsored fellowship program, Jennifer learned about the lack of books in schools that represent the diversity of Asian cultures. As a third-year teacher at a Philadelphia public charter school, students frequently asked her questions like, "Are you from China?" and "Where are you *really* from?" Her students' questions mirrored those she had been asked many times by her young classmates while growing up in the United States. As a child, she never saw books that reflected her culture. When she began to teach, Jennifer continued to notice the limited representation of Asian cultures in her school's curriculum:

> When looking solely at the curriculum, it's been the same since I was a child. Textbooks still only highlight the Western narrative. Our education system has solely focused on American history. The only times that Asian cultures are mentioned—such as Vietnam, Korea, Japan, and other countries of Asia—are when the United States "saves" them from warfare or colonizes them.

Frustrated with the primarily Western narrative in textbooks and in the curriculum, Jennifer felt the need to broaden her students' understandings about people who looked like her and those from other marginalized communities. She set aside one period per day to engage students in this work.

Jennifer first introduced her students to a central component of Vietnamese culture—the *áo dài,* which is a traditional Vietnamese garment. Her students expressed interest in the topic, but when she tried to find an age-appropriate book that captured the history and importance of the áo dài she discovered that none existed. When she couldn't find texts to educate her students about Vietnamese culture while challenging their preconceptions about AAPI communities, a lightbulb went off. Jennifer decided to write her own children's books, as she explained:

> I have been inspired to write and illustrate children's books that are not only mirrors for the Vietnamese community, but also windows for other children to learn. I see my first book, *My First Áo Dài,* as a way to educate others about the most significant garment in Vietnamese culture. The áo dài reflects the pride and beauty of Vietnam. It is part of my identity—it represents who I proudly am and I want my students, and students everywhere, to know about it. I want students who grew up like me, who look like me, and who have been frustrated like me to embrace their identities and to be proud of who they are.

Jennifer took a very personal approach to introducing the book in class, indicating that it was a reflection of her own identity, not just Ms. Dang (Jennifer) as their teacher, but Ms. Dang as a human who was once a little girl in school trying to figure out where she fit in. She modeled vulnerability and openness with her students by talking about the personal experiences that motivated her to write the book. As Jennifer read the book aloud, she encouraged her students to think about a part of themselves that people might overlook or not understand and write narratives about these themes. Jennifer used these stories to launch an author series where students wrote and illustrated their own books about being misunderstood as a way to challenge stereotypes and help readers to see beyond superficial dimensions of people. Moving from critical reading to action exemplifies two dimensions of Lewison et al.'s (2002) framework: disrupting the commonplace and taking action to promote social justice.

Jennifer shows us how she addressed a void in the curriculum by creating her own text that disrupted a commonplace assumption among many American elementary school students that all people who look like her are Chinese. She used her first book to dismantle the "perpetual foreigner/where-are-you-from?" syndrome that she and others from this community routinely face. Jennifer lived by the creed: *If you can't find it, create it.* We recognize that for many teachers, creating books and materials is an especially ambitious path toward advocacy-focused teaching, but anyone can use the Internet to find narratives and testimonials written by members of specific cultural communities. We could also consider inviting caregivers to share their heritage stories in our classrooms or assist us in creating digital curated text sets that feature their heritage and experiences to disrupt commonplace assumptions about communities.

Other teachers in our graduate network have used critical literacy in various ways, including Andrea from the last chapter. Let's take a closer look at how she uses texts to help students question commonplace assumptions, interrogate multiple perspectives, explore sociopolitical issues, and take action to promote social justice.

REVISITING ANDREA

Andrea regularly prompts her students to interrogate multiple viewpoints while discussing books (Lewison et al., 2002). She questions students about what perspective an author is writing from, what their identities are, and how these might be revealed in their books. For example, using the book *The Hunger Games* (Collins, 2008), Andrea invited students to consider how the book would change if its author had been a person of color or someone of another gender. She explained:

> We had a conversation about how *The Hunger Games* are representative of life in our own society. We talked about how the author is a white female named Suzanne Collins, and how her identity might get represented in a book . . . and how the book, and the representation of society, might be different if the author came from a different racial or gendered background. So, I try to do that every time I read a book. I feel like that's always an important thing to talk about: *What is their perspective? Why is the author writing from that perspective? Who is represented? Who is not? Why might that be the case?*

According to Andrea, questions such as these foster students' awareness of multiple perspectives and realities. She notes that students are often told or taught how to regurgitate answers in classrooms, but she sees how much they grow as critical thinkers when they are challenged to think about alternative perspectives. She also finds students to be highly engaged when they explore these types of questions.

Andrea positions herself as an "open book" with her students. She routinely discusses her white identity and blind spots, models her vulnerability, and encourages her students to do the same. She also holds students accountable for their ideas, which she considers to be a key part of building trusting relationships with them. Cognizant that her perceptions about texts are shaped by her whiteness, Andrea works with students to scrutinize the racialized nature of text messages through sharing critiques of books and other texts that reflect nondominant perspectives. For instance, she shared a time when she introduced her students to a critical review of the musical *Hamilton* while discussing the Revolutionary War:

> I pulled in an article critiquing *Hamilton* actually. Sure, everybody loves *Hamilton*, but one of the things I worry about, especially as a white educator, is my own bias and what I might not be seeing. . . .what I might not see in myself. So, I try, as much as possible, to bring in different, often critical, perspectives through all kinds of literacy sources, whether it be a book or a play or an editorial article or a news source.

The article she used with students critiqued how the Founding Fathers were made to seem honorable in the play and how aspects of slavery were overlooked. Andrea's students agreed that the criticism was justified (*Hamilton* creator Lin-Manuel Miranda has himself acknowledged the same), but they wanted to separate the glorification of the Founding Fathers and the historical inaccuracies in the musical from their overall appreciation for the innovative way history was presented through hip-hop music. Andrea hoped these critical explorations of *Hamilton* would shape the ways students consume social media. She observed that her students' perspectives have become distorted from spending so much time consuming information from the Internet. She explained:

> So often they'll tell me things and I'm just floored. I'm like, "Well, that's not true." And they'll push back that it was true because it was on TikTok. So, we talk about what's entertainment versus what we can consider news and we talk about how it's not that we can't learn from entertainment, but we need to be careful and critical consumers of information. And I talk to them about how news articles are different from social media posts. With social media, I address it like, "This is just a person who thinks this way." I want them to think critically and to know the difference between a person just posting because they feel like it versus a person who has done the research and would be considered an expert.

Andrea not only invites students to scrutinize social media, but also has students compose thought profiles of book characters and topics using Google Classroom. She feels such literacy events not only mirror students' interests, but also develop their composition abilities.

In this section, we have shared how Jennifer and Andrea invited students' critical readings of texts. Critical readings set students up for engaging in social action. Next, we will explore how to connect students to coalitions of highly dedicated individuals, groups, and organizations that are working to undo inequitable and unjust practices that adversely impact marginalized communities.

YOUTH AND EDUCATOR ACTIVISM

Student activism often begins with critical literacy, which affords students the opportunity to scrutinize issues and ideas contained in all types of texts. Through these engagements, students become immersed in studying more about an idea or issue, and engaged in solving real-world problems through the power of their own words and creations. In this section, we focus on examples of teachers and students tackling local problems by participating in what we call *action activism*. Action activism occurs when students see a problem, a challenge, or an injustice and they mobilize to address it, often with the support of advocacy-focused educators. We begin this discussion by going back to Cecilia's classroom.

REVISITING CECILIA

A few years back, Cecilia noticed that her students were really struggling with the impact of gun violence on their community. Being an educator–advocate, Cecilia sought out resources to support them and found a local nonprofit called *Need Indeed. Need Indeed* is a youth organization dedicated to helping students in grades 3–8 solve problems within their communities. The program partners with teachers, but the projects are all student-driven. Students explore multiple issues, select one to address through civic discourse (debates and voting), and they generate questions they would like answered. *Need Indeed* then provides speakers, articles, videos, and literature to support students on their quest for answers. Students refine their questions based on the information the organization provides and ultimately design and implement a unique project. Cecilia explains:

> Every student in my 5th-grade class knows someone personally who was a victim of gun violence. As a result, my class decided (after much research and debate) to study the issue this year, in conjunction with a nonprofit organization that helps young students in grades 3–8 research social justice subjects and aids them in finding ways to solve their chosen issue. We started out by brainstorming what we knew about gun violence and what questions we had. We also made a list of people with whom we wanted to speak. At first, students were interested in the police brutality aspect of gun violence, but after a visit from the supervisor of the Philadelphia Police Academy, the class decided to look more into gun reform in Philadelphia and the state of Pennsylvania. We are currently working to have a member of the city council visit us. By the end of the school year, my students will develop a service-learning project to benefit the school or the community at large.

Cecilia's classes have studied gun violence . . . twice. They've also explored topics like animal cruelty, drug use, and climate change. In Cecilia's classroom, students' lives, questions, and concerns became the curriculum. Her students used literacy to probe problems in their own communities and they explored how they could be part of the solution, an example of *action activism* in practice. Students' agentive work was precipitated by Cecilia's goal to create young activists, as she stated: *It is crucial that my students do this work and become social activists at such a young age because it lets them see the power they have to change the world.*

Cecilia teaches us that authentic learning begins with students' questions and direct engagements with community members to explore issues that concern them, such as the issue of gun violence. Her students' questions were the focal point for pursuing relevant knowledge about this topic, a notion that aligns with *intellect,* a valued tenet of the Black literary societies that Gholdy Muhammad (2020) describes. In these societies, members actively pursued knowledge about the world.

MEET BURTON

Burton is another teacher in our graduate program who has shown us what youth *and* educator activism looks like. Burton was one of a handful of Black teachers at a private K–12 residential school. Less than twenty percent of the student body at the school identified as students of color. Burton described an anti-racism campaign that took place at his school during the height of the Black Lives Matter (BLM) movement. He recalled the days after the murder of George Floyd, when racist graffiti appeared at a few school locations. School leaders responded by holding a school-wide assembly to condemn the graffiti and asked that teachers discuss the incident with students. They also sent letters home to caregivers explaining the school's response. Despite these efforts, student and teacher morale remained low. Several students felt school administrators had not adequately acknowledged issues of systemic racism that were being made transparent by the Black Lives Matter movement. They planned a silent day-long protest that would involve sitting quietly in class and not participating in any classroom discussions. Word of the protest reached school leaders who warned students about the ramifications for students resisting classroom activities.

Just prior to the protest, a few of Burton's students checked in with him. While he wanted students to know that he fully supported their cause, he also needed to maintain his faculty position. He explained:

> When rumblings of the pending protest were going on, a couple students came to my office and said "Mr. Burton, you are going to narc us out?" I couldn't help but laugh. I stressed to them the importance of doing something that they would be proud to be a part of. I asked them not to include me in their plans. I knew they had stuff on social media, so I suggested that they make sure not to

> use anything that used the school's image. I also explained to them that there is a certain level of power for them doing it as a student body without the involvement of the administration.

That afternoon, the majority of Burton's students engaged in the protest. He recalled: *I can't begin to express the level of pride I felt as a BIPOC educator/parent witnessing 23 of my 27 homeroom students engaging in the protest.* In reflecting on this act, Burton thought about his role as a teacher–activist. Raised in a family that spoke out against injustice, he believed he should extend these rights to his students:

> I grew up amongst very strong people in my family, so this notion of "I'm not giving up" (and) "I'm willing to fight for my rights" is nothing new to me and I was encouraged to do so. So, it's important for me to support my students in the same way. They need to know that I have their backs. As educators, particularly educators of color, I think it's important for students to feel encouraged to engage in peaceful protests or exercise their political rights.

Burton's students' protest galvanized faculty to educate students about the civil rights protests that precipitated the BLM movement and to create spaces for students to voice their outrage over police brutality and other racial injustices. The teachers responded by working collaboratively to create an interdisciplinary and multimodal curriculum to address systemic racism through English/language arts and history/social studies instruction. The curriculum focused on nonviolent civil rights protests, and it included the *Eyes on the Prize* series, the 1963 March on Washington D.C., the 1995 Million Man March, and several other films and podcasts. Faculty also created purposeful literacy-based assignments around these historical events. Burton found this work to be very meaningful. He reminisced:

> It was very emotional for all of us, but it was important. We created assignments like having them write speeches as if they were asked to be a speaker for the BLM movement. We encouraged them to express themselves in any way they wanted to. Kids wrote poems or performed spoken word, lyrics for songs, made drawings. Some even decided to express themselves in creative attire. The goal was just for them to find their voice and proudly express themselves. My hope was that they would have a meaningful experience. "I've shown you what successful social movements look like. . . . Use that as the foundation for whatever it is you're planning to do." And you know what? They did! They had a "speak out" and made a public pledge to say no to racism. The result was a campus climate of important and meaningful dialogue. I was proud of them!

In Burton's view, not only did the revised school curricula advance students' understandings of the history of nonviolent resistance to racial injustice, it helped hone their communication abilities so they could participate meaningfully in the BLM movement. Burton's case shows the transformative power of reorienting literacy curricula around interdisciplinary, justice-focused goals.

Burton's work with his students and colleagues reflects Paulo Freire's orientation to education and literacy in *Pedagogy of the Oppressed,* a book that was first translated into English in 1970. Freire, the founder and champion of critical pedagogy and one of the most influential educational thinkers of the 20th century, believed that educators should not be politically neutral. Deeply influenced by his experiences teaching and working in Brazil, Freire called for teachers to rally their students to critically examine power structures and patterns of inequality, and this call has resonated globally (Freire, 1973). In the United States, educators like Cecilia and Burton have become a driving force for social change both inside and outside of classrooms by involving their students in social action work. We recognize that establishing such campaigns can be difficult, especially with little in the way of school support. This is why Cecilia contacted the group *Need Indeed,* because this organization had already established an infrastructure to lend support to her so she could engage students in action activism.

You can do this, too. There are many ways you can link with organizations in your community to engage students in action activism. It's a win-win. Your students will be learning new vocabulary; spelling sophisticated words; reading new texts; writing letters; and drafting, revising, and editing speeches and podcasts. In other words, they will be advancing their literate capacities in order to solve community problems. Let's take a look at how you might connect with these types of organizations.

CONNECTING WITH ESTABLISHED ORGANIZATIONS

At global, national, state, and local levels, educators today are immersing themselves in groups and organizations that are working to better the circumstances in their schools and communities and to improve outcomes for their students and families. Organizations such as Black Lives Matter at School (https://www.blacklivesmatteratschool.com/) and the National Network of Teacher Activist Groups (https://teacheractivists.org/) are two national activist groups that aim to raise educators' awareness about racial justice campaigns and provide resources to help them take social campaigns into schools and communities. For example, BLM at School's website keeps educators informed about proposed legislation across the country that would prevent educators from teaching about racism, sexism, heterosexism, and oppression throughout U.S. history. The website offers curriculum resources, teacher testimonials, legislation updates, historical readings, and a link to the Zinn Education Project that includes a #TruthBeTold flipbook presented by the African American Policy Forum (AAPF, 1996;

#TruthBeToldTeam). The flipbook, which can be shared with students, details the right-wing war on critical race theory and what students, educators, and educational stakeholders can do about it.

Then there are local organizations we can look to, like Philly Children's Movement (PCM, https://phillychildrensmovement.org/), that work directly with educators, students, and caregivers to promote anti-racist work and mutual aid campaigns. To support 4th-grade students at Samuel Powell Elementary School in West Philadelphia, for example, PCM worked with other organizations to sponsor students' efforts to study gun violence and legislation. Students held a march against gun violence in their neighborhoods and then went to Harrisburg to ask Pennsylvania's legislators to vote for background checks for all gun purchases and require stolen guns to be reported to the police. Two weeks later, the students marched to Philadelphia City Hall with signs they designed, shouting chants that they composed, including:

> *"Hey, hey, ho, ho! All the guns have got to go!"*
> *"I want a LONGER life! I want a BETTER life! I want a GUN-FREE life!"*
> *"I matter. You matter. We Matter. Guns don't matter!"*

We also recognize local activists who are focused on developing, participating in, and leading projects locally and nationally in support of a more equitable and just education system. Seeing a need, and stepping into action, these groups rally around many of the issues that make schools alienating and unwelcoming places for BIPOC students. From research projects to petitions, from nonprofits to public–private partnerships, from classrooms to city hall, we see people from all walks of life getting involved to create more equitable and just education systems, and greater and more inspired opportunities, for children and youth. The breadth of the work is extraordinary, and its impact cannot be overstated.

In every community, and all over the world, there are organizations that engage students in action activism. While we have named a few local to our area, we hope you consider organizations in your own community that you might be interested in partnering with. At the global and national levels, we also want to recognize the work of these youth-led organizations and campaigns:

- Changemaker Xchange (https://changemakerxchange.org/)
- Global Girlhood (https://www.globalgirlhood.org/)
- The Black Knowledge Coalition (https://www.blackknowledgecoalition.org/)
- The Empathy Alliance (https://www.theempathyalliance.org/)
- DoSomething.Org (https://www.dosomething.org/us)
- Asians Speak Up (https://asiansspeakup.org/)
- Women Everywhere Believe (https://www.womeneverywherebelieve.org/)

- The Next Gen Come Up (https://www.thenextgencu.com/)
- #1000BlackGirlBooks (https://www.marleydias.com/1000blackgirlbooks/)
- United We Dream (https://unitedwedream.org/)
- Team ENOUGH (https://www.teamenough.org/)
- Future Coalition (https://futurecoalition.org/)

The issues faced by students and educators in our schools are often a reflection of the challenges faced by our communities. Like youth and teacher activism, community activism led by grassroots organizations is a hallmark of social change at the local level. Like many civically minded cities battling significant systemic forces and power structures, Philadelphia has a vibrant grassroots community. Every day, we see ordinary Philadelphians—like those who are angered by the staggering toll of gun violence on our youth, those whose families have been devastated by the impact of opioids, and those who are tired of wondering if ICE agents are coming for their loved ones—banding together to become forces for these causes, and many more. We see, and recognize, an endless legion of block captains, neighborhood associations, and community organizers mobilizing, meeting, protesting, fundraising, and campaigning to protect, empower, and support themselves, one another, and our city's children. These types of organizations also exist in your community, whether you are aware of them or you are not . . . yet. In the spirit of social change, we encourage you research, reach out, and connect with these groups.

Pause and Reflect

1. What do you know about youth and educator activism in your home or work community? Take inventory by exploring the efforts of activists in your area.
2. What are local activism opportunities that interest you most? How might you support or get involved in this work? Are there opportunities to connect students, families, and colleagues with these organizations?

CONCLUSION

We began this chapter by focusing on critical literacy, an orientation that invites readers to question texts that represent particular perspectives and realities. We can help students question all kinds of texts—from books to blogs, from Twitter posts to TikTok videos, from films to podcasts—no messages are off limits to critical scrutiny. Students can, and should, explore commonplace assumptions, dominant and missing voices, and issues of power and injustice. Only then can they formulate thoughtful positions on heavy issues. Participation in a democracy demands that we educate students to do these things, as they are constantly bombarded by conflicting and truth-bending messages. We have also described how to work with students to use their voices in powerful ways. The reality is that our students are, and can be, very capable agents of change. Whether it's a silent act of protest, a bullhorn in the auditorium, or the formation of a student union, our students have the right to be heard on issues that impact their lives and the world. They can transform our classrooms, our schools, our communities, and the future, but they need to be shown the way.

We have not ignored the fact that in an increasing number of states, teachers are not only barred from using texts such as Christine Leung's *What I See: Anti-Asian Racism from the Eyes of a Child,* they are prohibited from discussing any texts in ways that raise students' understandings about issues such as racism, gender identity, and sexuality. We know that the massive, multi-state legislative effort to restrict which texts teachers can use and how they can use them might leave you wondering whether critical teaching is even possible for you. In the next chapter, we will address what some educators are doing to confront this anti-intellectual movement. We will also check in with you about where you are in your development as an advocacy-focused teacher.

Recommended Books

- *Generation Brave: The Gen Z Kids Who Are Changing the World* (Alexander, 2020)
- *Marley Dias Gets It Done: And So Can You!* (Dias, 2018)
- *All Boys Aren't Blue: A Memoir-Manifesto* (Johnson, 2020)
- *Rebel Girls: Youth Activism and Social Change Across the Americas* (Taft, 2010)
- *How to Be a (Young) Antiracist* (Kendi & Stone, 2023)
- *Youth to Power: Your Voice and How to Use It* (Margolin & Thunberg, 2020)

CHAPTER 8

Pathways Toward Advocacy-Focused Teaching

> To bring about change, you must not be afraid to take the first step.
> We will fail when we fail to try.
>
> —Rosa Parks

As you read about the teachers in Chapters 6 and 7, did you see yourself in this work? By reading, reflecting on, and grappling with the issues raised in this book (and in other equity and advocacy-focused texts, films, podcasts, etc.) and by seeing your future self in the teacher profiles that we have shared, you have already taken a huge step. In this chapter, we offer guidance for extending your growth journey, even if you are working in school contexts that limit your authority. The chapter ends by addressing some grapple-worthy questions that can help you continue to learn and grow as an advocacy-focused literacy teacher.

Each community of practice offers particular affordances for teacher growth. If you are a full-time student of education, you might be able to participate in late-night discussions about racism with peers, but you have limited authority to change school curricula. Alternatively, if you are a practicing teacher, you have regular communication with students, caregivers, fellow teachers, and school leaders, but may be too focused on the immediacy of your work to deal with the inequities that are festering in your classroom or school. Given these conditions, let's look at how you might continue your journey as an advocacy-focused literacy teacher.

NOTICING INEQUITIES AND ENVISIONING CHANGE

Whether you are a full-time teacher candidate or a practicing teacher, there is much you can do to connect issues of equity, literacy, and language. Despite apprentices' limited access to students and schools, we have found that focused observations and journaling about equity help students advance their thinking about their advocacy roles.

On our campus, teacher candidates explore literacy instruction from an equity stance by reading research-based studies of literacy practice and relating their findings to observations of children in literacy classrooms. In their apprenticeship school sites, they engage in teacher noticing (Patterson Williams et al., 2019), which involves attending to and interpreting what they observe through a lens of equity and imagining how they might respond in more equitable ways to what they observe. Specifically, they are invited to take note of instances that appear to reduce or limit students' access to learning and reflect on these instances through an equity lens. They ask: *Do students seem engaged in learning? Are they connecting with their peers and the teacher? Do they take risks? Do they show joy for learning? Do they see themselves in the curriculum, on the walls of their classroom, and in the hallways of their school?* A focus on these elements of investigation leads to productive discussions about inequities in literacy classrooms and schools and how to dismantle them. We will share a few examples of these investigations.

Katie was a junior undergraduate education major who studied the significance of differentiated phonics instruction (Bear et al., 2020) and recognized that targeting instruction too far below or above students' zones of development (Vygotsky, 1978) would do little to advance their literacy growth. While at her internship placement, she observed the undifferentiated use of the district's frequently used phonics program. In her observational log, she captured how the use of this program appeared to work against the students who had already mastered the phonics skills being taught:

> I think that this was not necessarily equitable to all students as there were many who had already mastered the sounds she was reviewing. These students were not paying as much attention and distracting those who did not know the sounds. This was not beneficial to anyone and could have been approached in a better way that would best suit all the students. This could be done by pulling students who were having difficulty with these sounds in a small group during SSR time while other students are benefitting from independent reading.

It is possible not only to notice and name inequities in the literacy classroom, but also to imagine how you might address them. In one of our literacy education courses, candidates read the article "Closely Reading 'Reading Closely'" (Aukerman & Chambers Schuldt, 2016), which questions the practice of encouraging communal responses to texts. A communal response involves steering all students toward the same "correct" text response. For example, a typical, standards-based question in response to reading a narrative text would be: *What is the lesson of this story?* The "correct" answer might be identified in the curriculum guide that teachers are asked to follow. There may, however, be other justifiable responses to this question that are not identified in the curriculum guide, based on the evidence provided in the text and students' experiences and understandings about the world. One of our apprentice teachers, Jessica, explored equity by looking closely at the ways her host teacher, Ms. Flynn, facilitated discussions about texts. Jessica admired much about Ms. Flynn's teaching, but noted an occasion where she felt her host teacher limited students' thinking about a text. She captured this observation in her field log:

> The class read a story yesterday and today they were answering questions about that story. The teacher asked the question, "What was the lesson of this story?" and many students raised their hands. The first student she called on said the lesson of the story was that hard work pays off, which was correct. The teacher stated that this was correct, praised him, and she said, "You took the words right out of my mouth." Then, she asked all of the students, "Who else thought this was the lesson of the story?" and almost everyone raised their hands.

In reflecting on this instance, Jessica concluded that by praising one student's "correct" response, Ms. Flynn had prevented others from formulating their own potentially plausible interpretations. To Jessica, this move short-changed thinking possibilities for most of the students in the class—an instructional action that she tagged as inequitable. The investigation also enabled her to imagine how she would change this practice if she had a chance to do so:

> If this were my classroom, I would not have stated that the first student was correct. Instead, I would say, "That's a great idea," and I would ask him for text evidence to support his idea. Then, I would open the question up to students again to hear their varied perspectives. I don't think all students were thinking the same thing; rather, I think they just wanted to say that they did to please the teacher and move on. Therefore, by having all students share their ideas, they would engage in discourse and practice supporting their ideas with text evidence. This is an example of a close communal reading where the teacher has a specific answer in her mind, and students try to cater their thinking to fit the teacher's.

In this entry, Jessica identified herself as a teacher who would invite students to construct and defend text interpretations using text evidence, a practice she associated with equitable literacy teaching.

The equity-focused investigations that Althier invited in her literacy courses were precipitated by reflecting on current literacy scholarship. Apprentices were asked to apply their emerging perspectives to consider whether students were learning, being heard, or being seen. These investigations allowed candidates to envision ways to make literacy learning more equitable. Although Katie and Jessica lacked the authority to change the teaching practices or curriculum in their apprenticeship schools, they developed dispositions that would prepare them to act in accord with their beliefs in their own future classrooms (Lazar, 2022). Let's take a break now to consider how you might investigate classroom inequities that limit students' literacy growth.

PAUSE AND REFLECT

1. In the schools you visit or work in, what normalized routines for literacy learning might actually be inequitable for some students?
2. What state-, district-, or school-level policies seem to undermine students' literacy learning?

NOTICING INEQUITIES AND FORGING CHANGE

Practicing teachers are positioned to forge real change in their classrooms and schools, although possibilities for enacting teacher authority are varied, and dependent on a number of factors. Cecilia and Andrea are in public schools with a mandated curriculum but have been able to create equitable, safe, and culturally sustaining spaces for learning in their classrooms. They are also well-established educators who feel empowered to work against structures and practices that undermine their students' achievement. Recall that Cecilia changed her social studies curriculum to emphasize Black achievement and Andrea stood her ground to keep Cardi B's quotations on the walls of her classroom.

Not everyone, however, feels secure enough to push back against the overwhelming presence of whiteness in the curriculum or stand up to colleagues who disagree with their advocacy stances. Most teachers have little say in the types of literacy programs that their districts adopt. What can you do when your district has just spent millions of dollars on a new reading program that you find out of sync with students' lives, experiences, and learning needs? Such a problem seems immutable to change, even for experienced teachers. Further, the isolation often associated with the teaching profession exacerbates teachers' feelings of helplessness.

One pathway for developing teacher agency is practitioner inquiry, a stance that positions teachers as knowers and agents for educational reform (Cochran-Smith & Lytle, 2009). Practitioner inquiry is especially powerful when teachers join with their colleagues to inquire about matters of educational equity in professional learning communities (PLCs). PLCs have traditionally involved "teachers working collaboratively in school-based groups to examine student and school data in order to take collective responsibility for students' learning" (Cochran-Smith & Lytle, 2009, p. 49). They may collaborate in theme-related work to discuss, for example, specific elements of literacy practice and its impact, based on reviews of students' artifacts, observational notes of teaching practices, recordings of their own or others' practices, as well as test scores and other site documents.

Teachers may also use PLCs to examine how top-down prescriptive mandates impact students' literacy development, engagement in learning, risk-taking abilities, and identification with school. For instance, the collaborative work done in two different Philadelphia-based PLCs provided a space for teachers to develop their own counter-mandates that directly challenged prescriptive curricula being imposed on them (Crawford-Garrett & Riley, 2016). Group members justified the use of more critical, culturally centered teaching, based on their experiences of having their own heritage erased in school, wanting to exercise their identities as social activists, and being exposed to alternative texts that showed them how equity work could be done in schools. These groups offered safe and nurturing spaces to "define and redefine social justice and their identities as social justice educators within and against their school contexts" (p. 44).

We can imagine teachers coming together in these groups to take stock of their school climates with questions like: *Are our teaching practices, curricula, and schools fostering equitable or inequitable practices, structures, and routines? How do we know? What inequitable practices, structures, and routines might be invisible because they are so normalized in literacy classrooms?* We also envision PLCs exploring the possibilities of equity within literacy classrooms by asking: *How can we examine and use students' funds of knowledge to rethink standards and make teaching culturally sustaining? How can we bring community wealth into the classroom to broaden what counts as literacy?* We can also imagine PLCs that include caregivers and community-based activists who could contribute insights about cultural values and practices, community aspirations, and issues critical to communities. Such inquiry groups can enhance teacher knowledge and capacity to make equity-focused changes to curriculum and instruction that advance students' learning and support their social–emotional needs (Leonard & Woodland, 2022).

What is most difficult is when teachers work in educationally conservative schools, districts, or states where the mention of particular topics could get a teacher reprimanded or fired. This is the case with Kristin, one of our former students, who was able to advocate for her students, but only to a point. We will use her case to discuss possible pathways for advocacy when options seem very limited.

MEET KRISTIN

Kristin is a white, second-year teacher who teaches in a 2nd-grade parochial school that primarily serves students who recently immigrated from Nigeria and other West African nations. Kristin attributes her advocacy-focused work to our teacher education program's many opportunities to reflect on issues of equity, as she stated, *because of all the reflecting that we did and the time that we spent on culturally appropriate teaching, I went into so many classrooms for field experience where I was able to reflect and think about what I would keep the same or what I would change in my own classroom.*

As a novice teacher in a small parochial school, Kristin feels almost completely alone in the work of translating the idea of culturally centered teaching into practices that are fit for her students. She has turned to other teachers, particularly teachers of color via Instagram, to learn specific ways to create a culturally welcoming classroom. The teachers Kristin follows on Instagram discuss the importance of getting students' names right on the first day of school as a way to preserve their identities and establish a community of learners. Kristin took note of how they were using literature in their classrooms, and found a teacher who used the book *Your Name Is a Song* (Thompkins-Bigelow, 2020). On the first day of school, Kristin used the book to welcome her students.

Your Name Is a Song details how a young girl named Kora Jalimuso comes home one day from school complaining that no one could pronounce her name, not even her teacher. The girl's mother enlightens her daughter about the beauty, pronunciation, and origins of African American, African, Middle Eastern, and Latinx names. Included in the text are phonetic translations of each name. The girl's mother sings each name, emphasizing its unique meaning and melodic sound combinations. The combined information is instructive and it provides powerful evidence that names are significant. For instance, Mother exclaims: "And Laquan (LAA-KWAN) and Lamika (Lah-MEE-Ka) are the twinkle in stars, the glimmer in minds that think and tinker." Note Thompkins-Bigelow's use of metaphors to connect these names with brilliance and creativity. The next day, the girl goes to school and finds that, again, her teacher is unable to pronounce her name. Turning this disappointment into an opportunity, the girl begins to sing the names of her teacher and classmates, as her mother taught her to do. Finally, the teacher invites her to sing the song of her own name.

Kristin describes how she used the book as a springboard to invite students to teach others about their names. She also talks about what this practice means to her in order to affirm students, families, and cultural communities:

> We talk about how names are super important and how names are important for me. And so then each student gets up, says their name, if they're comfortable, says their name in front of the class, and then I'll repeat it to make sure I'm saying it correctly. And I think that's super important on the very first day to ensure that, because names are usually culturally important, too, so that their culture is being honored, their family is being honored, their name is being honored throughout the whole year.

By inviting students to say their names, and ensuring she could accurately repeat them, Kristin not only affirmed students' cultural identities on Day 1, but also positioned students as teachers, and teachers on Instagram as teachers for us all. We now use this picture book on campus to show how literature can be used in culturally sustaining ways! What we have here is a continuous learning loop that involves children, teacher candidates, virtual teachers, and teacher educators—all sharing, constructing, and repurposing knowledge (Zeichner, 2009).

Kristin's attention to students' identities aligns with historically responsive teaching practices (Muhammad, 2020). She finds that identity is deeply entwined with literacy learning: "Before getting to literacy skill development such as decoding, fluency, comprehension, writing, or any other content-learning standards, students must authentically see themselves in the learning" (p. 69). Kristin's work also reminds us of Muhammad's (2020) dual focus on identities and skills in historically responsive literacy teaching.

As Kristin navigated her first 2 years in the classroom, she started to recognize, and deeply appreciate, the abundance of community cultural wealth surrounding her school. She observed:

> There is so much vibrancy and an abundance of non-financial wealth in my school community, which is really important to recognize. I do see the love that parents and families have for the school and for the teachers and for their kids. Most families are so grateful that their children are here and they will say it all the time to the teachers. There is an abundance of gratitude. A lot of the parents will—even though I know that they're struggling—they'll bring gifts for Christmas or they'll make sure that their kids bring in extra wipes, extra paper towels, stuff to make sure the classroom's fine. And then our principal really helps out a lot. She finds money in crazy places to help these parents with costs because she really feels like they should all be here and everyone should have a place in our school.

Kristin's appreciation of the caregivers and the community surrounding her school echoes what we address in our teacher education program about recognizing community wealth (Yosso, 2005).

While Kristin viewed her school's curriculum as expandable in the area of affirming students' racial and cultural identities, she was less inclined to address issues of sexual identification and orientation because she believed that these topics were still taboo at her religiously affiliated school. Kristin didn't view these identities as less than or undeserving of being part of the curriculum. However, because her principal was a nun and because students' parents chose religious education for various reasons, Kristin found herself in a difficult situation.

> Since I work for a parochial school, I try to work in, not just culturally diverse materials, but I have books about a little boy who wants to be a mermaid, and

> there's another book about a gay wedding. I think it's important for them to see, but it's pretty tricky.

We asked Kristin to talk more about her trepidation around using literature that addressed LGTBQIA+ issues. Kristin shared that when she interviewed with the school, her principal ended the interview with a cautionary tale about a teacher who was fired for living with her partner while unmarried. Kristin was never explicitly told then, or even since, there are issues or topics she cannot teach or touch upon, but she took that initial conversation to mean that educators at the school needed to uphold the beliefs of the religious institution both inside and outside of the classroom. We want to acknowledge the complex nature of Kristin's decision-making here. She hasn't been explicitly told not to recognize family diversity based on LGBTQIA+ identities, but if she does, would it come at a cost? A cost like . . . her job? That certainly seems to be the insinuation, albeit real or perceived, based on her comments.

We also recognize that Kristin is far from alone in navigating the cost of honoring LGBTQIA+ identities in the classroom. In Florida, for example, the instructions have been made clear: "Don't Say Gay." In many states other than Florida, including our home state of Pennsylvania, hotlines, legislation, and campaigns have been introduced to ban talk of gender, gender identity, sexual orientation, and transgender issues. We recognize these attempts as the fear of and/or hate for what is "other" . . . not-so-subtly disguised as concern for children. We see an agenda here, and it exists outside the scope of education. An equity-focused educational approach would be one that creates space to appreciate that there may be children who identify as LGBTQIA+ or who are starting to identify in these ways or whose families reflect these identities.

Back to Kristin. Whether the barriers to addressing issues of sexual identity in her classroom are real or perceived, Kristin felt limited in her capacity to advocate for all of her students and their families at this school. Her case raises questions about the compartmentalization of advocacy work. How can she so thoughtfully advocate for certain students while avoiding advocacy for others? In situations where we find ourselves unable to advocate for all students, we need to explore how educators in our own and other teaching communities approach the issue. In Kristin's case, she might pursue how teachers in other religiously affiliated schools grapple with locating issues of sexual identity in their teaching and curricula.

One takeaway from Kristin's story is that if you find yourself in a school with limited support to advocate for students, there are virtual learning communities that you can turn to. This is how she learned about Thompkins-Bigelow's book: *I followed teachers on social media (too) who shared a children's book called* Your Name Is a Song *and that book is what made me realize how important it was for me to get their names right.* Kristin's ability to turn thoughts into actions within a restrictive school setting reveals the power of virtual learning communities for teachers. We wondered if she could apply this same strategy to using books that featured LGBTQIA+ characters. We also wondered what would happen if she joined one or more of her colleagues to explore this possibility. We ask: *What would you do?*

We recognize that teachers in schools of all types are under increased scrutiny about what they can say and do. Public school teachers in an alarming number of states face possible dismissal if they talk about issues like systemic racism, sexual orientation, or gender identity. Not being able to talk about the makeup of students' families is a harming practice because it denies students their humanity. Not being able to discuss why so many Black people have been murdered or mistreated at the hands of police is a harmful practice because it keeps students in the dark about racist policing procedures and therefore limits their ability to advocate for justice. What are educators supposed to do? We suggest taking a layered approach. Day to day, we do what we've always done. We show up for our kids. We commit to making every classroom a safe space for every whole child. We honor students, families, and communities in our words, in our actions, in our pedagogical approaches, on our classroom walls, in our classroom libraries, and in our curricula. And in the bigger picture? We galvanize, we find each other, and we advocate. There is strength in numbers. Action activism, allyship, and professional learning communities will be instrumental in putting an end to these harmful practices. Let's continue the conversation by talking about next steps.

NEXT STEPS

This book does not tread lightly. It does not tiptoe around the issues, the challenges, and the barriers that educators face on a daily basis. Issues of equity can be difficult to talk about and challenging to take on. Still, we encourage you to do just that. Sit with these ideas, think about your responses throughout the book, and keep working at it. Ask yourself, how do these ideas and issues live within your mind? Within your heart? Within your teaching practice? Within your classroom? Within your communities, both home and work? Are there changes you want to make? Are there questions that you have? And of course, can you see a path forward to get you there?

YOUR PATH BEGINS WITH YOU

As we've shared, there is no magic spell that will transport us where we want to go. If we want to move the needle, we have to do the work, individually and collectively. Our first set of action steps speaks to practices or habits of mind that you may be engaged in or that you could engage in on your path toward advocacy-focused teaching. These practices start within and then grow outward.

We have identified some key areas for further study and reflection. It might be gratifying for you to work with others to find additional resources (books, articles, films, websites, podcasts, or social media resources) to explore these areas in greater depth. You might sustain these inquiries over time, gather and share insights, see how they are relevant for your own school communities, and report out what you discover. You might even consider contributing your insights and experiences to a publication, website, or blog.

Let's start by looking *inward*. To do this, we encourage you to:

Ask yourself how issues of race and culture live within you. In order to view all students through a capacity lens, you will need to engage in critical self-work. This means unpacking how your racial position and other cultural affiliations have shaped your opportunities and ways of seeing others. It is also about taking an honest look at the ways you have perpetuated racist ideas through your language and actions. By doing this kind of self-inventory, or excavation (Sealey-Ruiz, 2021), you will be positioned to interrupt racist structures that are embedded in schooling and society.

Think about your use of language, your words, and their impact. Your words matter. The words that you use to describe the children, families, and communities that you work with will have an impact on your approach to this work. It is critical to understand that there is language that empowers and recognizes the many strengths of marginalized people and communities and there is language that disempowers, erases, and minimizes those strengths. How do you describe the students, school, and community you work in? Does your use of language reflect the assets and abundance of wealth present within your students, their families, and their communities?

Now, let's look *outward*. To guide you, we recommend considering the practices recommended for educators by Ofelia García and Jo Anne Kleifgen (2018) in their book *Educating Emergent Bilinguals: Policies, Programs, and Practices for English Learners*, detailed as follows.

Study the context of your school community. As an advocacy-focused educator, it's important for you to become familiar with the communities in which children live. It's equally important to familiarize yourself with the "histories of the cultural practices in which children and youth are immersed at home and in the community" (García & Kleifgen, 2018, p. 174). A study for you might look like familiarizing yourselves with community organizations, programs, houses of worship, immigration patterns, and the like, that students might be connected to or attend.

Learn about your students and their families. You will want to expand your knowledge and understanding of every student you come across by paying attention to students' physical presence, including their gestures and facial expressions, as well as their behaviors and relationships with others (García & Kleifgen, 2018). It's important to see every child as a whole person. You also want to learn as much as you possibly can about and from the families of your students. Encourage parents, grandparents, caregivers, siblings—whoever may be at home—to participate in classroom activities. Invite them to share their cultural and linguistic histories and practices. Doing so is equally critical to helping families make sense of school structures, policies, and processes, and to invite them to provide feedback and offer ideas for alternatives.

Learn about the home literacy and language of your students. If your students don't use a standardized form of English or a language other than English, you'll want to learn about the dialects and home languages they do use. You can ask students to share with you, and you can talk to family members and community members about what you hear in your classroom. If students speak a language other than English, you might learn simple phrases or songs that you can share with the class. You can also ask families to share multilingual materials and devise your own classroom signage to reflect the dialects and languages represented (García & Kleifgen, 2018).

Observe and listen to your students. Your students are experts on their own lives. It's important to listen and observe them. You can listen to your students in the hallways, in the cafeteria, in the gym, before drop-off, at pickup, on the playground, and so on. You can also listen to your students' families in these settings or on special occasions. In addition, you'll want to pay attention to the environment. What's the signage around the school and in the community? Ask your students about the shows they watch, the music they listen to, the computer games they play, the social media platforms they use, the TikTok videos they love, and so on (García & Kleifgen, 2018). Listening and observing will build your understanding of their funds of knowledge.

ENVISION AND FORGE CHANGE

As you continue your journey, we encourage you to be honest with yourself about the strengths and the limitations of your teaching practice. It's never too early . . . or too late . . . to make your presence as an advocacy-focused educator known and to make your classroom a safe space for every child who enters it. Our second set of action steps draws your attention to some of the practices that underlie advocacy-focused teaching.

One of the first steps you can take to envision and forge change is to *set the tone for your classroom.* Here, again, we look to, and expand upon, the recommendations of García and Kleifgen (2018) by encouraging you to:

Celebrate and honor students' languages. Your classroom environment, and the message it sends to your students about their belonging, starts with you. Foster a classroom environment that helps students access standardized English, while honoring the diverse dialects and languages they use. You can and *should* help your students learn the rules, norms, and conventions of standardized English, preferably through writing, as they are expected to use this variation in school, but it shouldn't be the only language that they are welcome to use in school. Recognize the beauty of their languages, but also name, notice, and dismantle instances of linguistic violence that may be operating in your school.

Adopt inclusive pedagogical approaches such as translanguaging. Think of translanguaging as a political stance that you can take. Invite students to use their home language in a variety of ways for a variety of learning goals. You might invite students to use their home language while talking informally in peer groups to prepare for an exam. You might encourage them to take notes in their home language as you explain a concept in English (García & Kleifgen, 2018). Your students' language can't be checked at your classroom door. Your students *need* it to accomplish their learning goals. They will need to strengthen their multilingual abilities to flourish as citizens of diverse and global societies.

Welcome students to consider and study language practices. Invite your students to become linguists. Linguists are "comfortable analyzing language practices, developing metalinguistic skills, comparing named languages, thinking aloud about language, and critiquing the way languages are used in print and digital media, as well as in public life" (García & Kleifgen, 2018, p. 175). You can help your students become aware of the power of named languages in society and in schools by adopting or adhering to the frameworks discussed in Chapters 6 and 7.

Share your "why" as an advocacy-focused educator. You can and *should* talk to your students about your own convictions. Engage them in real talk about real issues that are relevant to your life and their lives. Talk to them about equity—what it means to you, what it means to them, and what it can look like when it is co-constructed in your classroom. Share with them your desire to build a more inclusive and just world. As you do, you can encourage them to do the same.

Another important step is to *plan and prepare* yourself, your classroom, and your curriculum. Drawing upon the work of Muhammad (2020) and García and Kleifgen (2018), we recommend that you:

Teach criticality. Teach criticality and infuse this way of thinking into your curricula. "When youth have criticality, they are able to see, name, and interrogate the world not only to make sense of injustice but also to work toward social transformation" (Muhammad, 2020, p. 120). You can push students to tell the difference between facts and truth and cultivate within them the tools to dismantle deficit ways of thinking. You can foster students as active interrogators rather than passive consumers of knowledge and information.

Provide a challenging curriculum with culturally affirming, historically responsive, and relevant material. You can adjust your curricula. A challenging curriculum is one that scaffolds rather than simplifies based on students' abilities, interests, and needs. You can infuse your lessons with materials, resources, and technology to help students access substantive information in their home languages. You can also invite students to research and locate material that they find both challenging and relevant (García & Kleifgen, 2018). By engaging in these practices, not only are you supporting them as capable young scholars, but you are also encouraging them to see themselves in this way.

Select texts that reflect the students and families in your classroom. When selecting texts for today's classrooms, you'll want to consider not only who is in your classroom, but also what you're teaching and how you plan to teach it. You'll want to select texts that enable the teaching of the curriculum, but also push students to critically analyze and drive positive identity development. Muhammad (2020) encourages educators to ask themselves questions when considering texts, such as: "Why did I choose this text to teach with [beyond the text being in the mandated curriculum]? Have my students contributed to the selection of texts for teaching and learning? How will this text advance my students' learning of identity of themselves or other people/cultures? How will this text advance my students' learning or skills and intellects?" (p. 145).

Meet your students where they are, as they are. You can meet students where they are, as they are, because you know where they've been. You may have students in your classroom whose literacy practices have been disrupted by violence, genocide, political unrest, famine, natural disasters, and other very real social conditions. These students will have different needs than those who may be sitting next to them speaking the very same dialect or home language. You need to recognize these differences, should they exist, and be aware of these realities and their impact. "Educators need to be aware of these differences and provide students with appropriate lessons and pedagogy" (García & Kleifgen, 2018, p. 176).

Embrace the writing process. The iterative process inherent to writing—the brainstorming, the drafting, the editing, and so on—lends itself to being a kind, gentle, and engaging literacy practice. You can offer students all kinds of diverse opportunities to experience, experiment, and practice with the English language in rich and diverse ways through writing. Your students can write across many different genres. You can invite them to explore, investigate, create, and share on their own or with peers. They can write for you or for a broader audience. From autobiographies to poetry to social media posts, the process of writing can help you understand your students in unique ways while also supporting your students on own their literacy journeys.

Appreciate what your students know, and build upon that foundation. If your kindergarteners do not know the alphabet, if your 3rd-graders can't multiply, if your 5th-graders have a limited understanding of the government, if your 8th-graders have little prior knowledge of properties of matter, or your high school students haven't had any exposure to a foreign language, remind yourself to think about how these standards are a social construction, built around the literacies and competencies of the culturally dominant. It's important to learn to see a child's inability to meet grade expectations as a consequence of unequal and inhumane schooling rather than an inherent flaw in their own ability or character. Instead of blaming students and their caregivers for failing to prepare for the standards of the grade level, help students develop knowledge by drawing from the literacies, languages, knowledge, and interests that they bring to the classroom.

Our book is about advocacy and what we'd like to leave you with is a call to action. We invite you to think about the people, the places, the spaces, the ways, and the means of your advocacy work. Ask yourself: Who's your who? What's your why? Where's your where? To that end, we encourage you to:

Engage in action activism. You can be an advocacy-focused teacher who engages in action activism. You can supplement what is required (curriculum, assessment) with innovative, culturally and historically relevant materials and practices based on your "own close observations, performance assessments, and professional judgments" (García & Kleifgen, 2018, p. 176). You can ensure your students are seen, heard, and represented, *as they are,* in your classrooms—and you can advocate for them, their families, and their communities, *as they are,* outside of their classrooms. Your job is to demonstrate a genuine love and respect for kids, but also to join your colleagues or other PLCs in scrutinizing and dismantling literacy curricula and schooling systems that exclude, silence, or simply "tolerate" students' literacies and languages (Bomer, 2021).

Seek out allies and professional learning communities. Know that you are not alone. You can find like-minded colleagues in your school or district, in faculty, in peers, or even in communities that exist online or through social media. We highlighted a few advocacy-oriented groups local to the Philadelphia area back in Chapter 7, and there are many more that we have come to know and appreciate. Wherever you are living and working, there will be advocates with websites and phone numbers and email addresses. We also listed a number of organizations operating at national and even global levels, and we encourage you to explore their work and to reach out. The beauty of this work lies in connection. Advocates welcome allies and thrive in PLCs.

PUTTING IT ALL TOGETHER

We began this book by pointing out how schools deny far too many students of color the experiences that would help them realize their fullest literacy potential. To make our point, we drew from Ta-Nehisi Coates's testimony of his public school education, which he associated with compliance and intellectual imprisonment. His love of words was nourished early on by family members who directed him to texts that would satisfy his boundless curiosity, which for a critical time period, focused on the origins of racism. We began this book by asking how it is that we cannot give these types of humane, critical, and culturally centered learning environments to all students?

While we know there are elements that conspire against students and their families that educators cannot directly control, there are things you can do to see and nurture students' fullest literacy capacities. We recommend that you extend your growth by studying more deeply the intersections between equity, literacy, and language. We have identified broad areas of study that will help you begin a journey toward becoming the advocacy-focused teacher that all students need. Your learning will be most meaningful if you can arrange to be in the company of educators who are already doing advocacy work in schools. Find an ally—someone you can bounce ideas off of, someone who can join you in trying out an idea that promotes learning and equity. Do not be afraid to invite conversations with school leaders. Now is the time for courageous conversations, and it will take bravery to support students' literate development.

Our purpose for this book was to point out the urgent need for all of us to do this work, and to give you enough anchoring in the professional literature and our own experiences in Philadelphia's schools for you to take these ideas into your own community, university, and life. Exploring concepts of culture, race, and intersectionality, literacies and languages as cultural practices, the sociology of schooling, and culturally and linguistically inclusive frameworks and practices, provides you with a wide-angle lens for beginning your journey. Kids everywhere are depending on you. We wish you the best of luck with your continued journey.

Recommended Resources

- *Anti-Defamation League: Creating an Anti-Bias Learning Environment (https://www.adl.org/)*
- *Center for Racial Justice in Education (https://centerracialjustice.org/)*
- *Crash Course: Black American History Preview (https://thecrashcourse.com/topic/bah/)*
- *Conscious Style Guide (https://consciousstyleguide.com/)*
- *Embrace Race (https://www.embracerace.org/)*

- *Learning for Justice (https://www.learningforjustice.org/)*
- *National Museum of African American History & Culture and The Smithsonian*
  - » *Black History Learning Lab Resources (https://learninglab.si.edu/org/nmaahc)*
  - » *Talking About Race (https://nmaahc.si.edu/learn/talking-about-race)*
- *The Race Institute for K–12 Educators (http://www.raceinstitute.org/)*
- *Say Their Names Toolkit from Chicago Public Schools (https://www.cps.edu/sites/equity/tools/me/say-their-names/)*
- *Social Justice Books: A Teaching for Change Project (https://www.teachingforchange.org/socialjusticebooks-org)*

References

Adams, D. W. (2020). *Education for extinction: American Indians and the boarding school experience, 1875–1928*. University Press of Kansas.

African American Policy Forum [AAPF]. (1996). https://www.aapf.org/truthbetold

Ahmed, S. (2012). *On being included: Racism and diversity in institutional life*. Duke University Press.

Alexander, M. (2013). *The new Jim Crow: Mass incarceration in the age of colorblindness*. The New Press.

Alim, H. S. (2016). *Raciolinguistics: How language shapes ideas about race*. Oxford University Press.

Allington, R. L. (2000). Effects of reading policy on classroom instruction and student achievement. *CELA Research Report*.

Almeida, L. (2021, August 6). *A history of racist federal housing policies*. Mass Budget. https://massbudget.org/2021/08/06/a-history-of-racist-federal-housing-policies/

Alvarez, A. & Milner, H. R., IV. (2018). Exploring teachers' beliefs and feelings about race and police violence. *Teaching Education, 29*(4), 383–394.

American Psychological Association [APA], Presidential Task Force on Educational Disparities. (2012). Ethnic and racial disparities in education: Psychology's contributions to understanding and reducing disparities. Retrieved from http://www.apa.org/ed/resources/racial-disparities.aspx.

Anderson, K. (2013). *Little Rock: Race and resistance at Central High School*. Princeton University Press.

Anderson, L. W. & Krathwohl, D. R. (2001). *A taxonomy for learning, teaching, and assessing: A revision of Bloom's taxonomy of educational objectives*. Pearson.

Anele, U. (2020). Anti-literacy laws in the United States once prevented Blacks from getting an education. Retrieved from https://talkafricana.com/anti-literacy-laws-in-the-united-states-once-prevented-black-men-from-getting-an-education/

Anyon, J. (2014). *Radical possibilities: Public policies, urban education, and a new social movement*. (2nd ed.). Routledge.

Au, K. H. P. (1980). Participation structures in a reading lesson with Hawaiian children: Analysis of a culturally appropriate instructional event. *Anthropology & Education Quarterly, 11*(2), 91–115.

Au, K. H. P. & Jordan, C. (1981). Teaching reading to Hawaiian children: Finding a culturally appropriate solution. *Culture and the Bilingual Classroom: Studies in Classroom Ethnography*, 139–152.

August, D. & Hakuta, K. (Eds.). (1997). *Improving schooling for language-minority children: A research agenda*. National Research Council, National Academic Press.

Aukerman M. & Chambers Schuldt, L. (2016). Closely reading "reading closely." *Language Arts, 93*(4), 286–299. https://www.jstor.org/stable/43824286?seq=1

Aukerman, M. & Chambers Schuldt, L. (2016). "The pictures can say more things": Change across time in young children's references to images and words during text discussion. *Reading Research Quarterly, 51*(3), 267–287.

Aukerman, M. & Chambers Schuldt, L. (2021). What matters most? Toward a robust and socially just science of reading. *Regarding Research Quarterly, 56*(S1), S85–S103.

Bailystok, E. (2007). Acquisition of literacy in bilingual children: A framework for research. *Language Learning, 57*(1), 45–77.

Baker-Bell, A. (2020). *Linguistic justice: Black language, literacy, identity, and pedagogy*. Routledge.

Balfanz, R., Byrnes, V. & Fox, J. (2014). Sent home and put off-track: The antecedents, disproportionalities, and consequences of being suspended in ninth grade. *The Journal of Applied Research on Children: Informing Policy for Children at Risk, 5*(2), Article 13.

Bear, D. R., Invernizzi, M., Templeton, S. & Johnston, F. (2020). *Words their way: Word study for phonics, vocabulary, and spelling instruction* (7th ed.). Pearson.

Bell, D. A. (1980). *Brown v. Board of Education* and the interest-convergence dilemma. *Harvard Law Review, 93*(3), 518–533.

Bell, D. A. (1995). Who's afraid of Critical Race Theory? *University of Illinois Law Review, 1995*(4), 893–910.

Berlin, I. (Producer). (2003). *Race: The power of an illusion*. Retrieved from California Newsreel.

Bishop, R. S. (1990). Mirrors, windows, and sliding glass doors. *Choosing and Using Books for the Classroom, 6*(3), 1–2.

Blumenbach, J. F. (1865). *The anthropological treatises of Johann Friedrich Blumenbach*. (T. Bendyshe, Trans.). Longman, Green, Longman, Roberts, and Green.

Boaler, J., Wiliam, D. & Brown, M. (2000). Students' experiences of ability grouping—Disaffection, polarisation and the construction of failure. *British Educational Research Journal, 26*(5), 631–648.

Bomer, K. (2010). *Hidden gems: Naming and teaching from the brilliance in every student's writing*. Heinemann.

Bomer, K. (2021). Leaving behind the "learning loss": Loving and learning from the ways students talk, write, and draw right now. *Language Arts, 98*(6), 352–359.

Borg, L. (2015, October 11). *Bridging the word gap for needy children*. The Providence Journal. https://www.providencejournal.com/story/news/education/2015/10/12/bridging-word-gap-for-needy/33284270007

Bottiani, J. H., Bradshaw, C. P. & Mendelssohn, T. (2017). A multilevel examination of racial disparities in high school discipline: Black and white adolescents' perceived equity, school belonging, and adjustment problems. *Journal of Educational Psychology, 109*, 532–545.

Boyd, M. P. & Markarian, W. C. (2011). Dialogic teaching: Talk in service of a dialogic stance. *Language and Education, 25*(6), 515–534.

Buffon, G. L. L. (1853). Of the apparent varieties of the human species. In *Buffon's natural history of man, the globe, and of quadrupeds* (pp. 118–156). Leavitt & Allen.

Carter, P. L. & Welner, K. G. (2013). *Closing the opportunity gap: What America must do to give every child an even chance.* Oxford University Press.

Castro, A. J. (2010). Themes in the research on preservice teachers' views of cultural diversity: Implications for researching millennial preservice teachers. *Educational Researcher, 39*, 198–210.

Cervetti, G., Pardales, M. J. & Damico, J. (2001). A tale of differences: Comparing the traditions, perspectives, and educational goals of critical reading and critical literacy. *Reading Online, 4*(9).

Charity Hudley, A. H. & Mallinson, C. (2010). *Understanding English language variation in U.S. schools.* Teachers College Press.

Cherry-Paul, S., Reynolds, J., Kendi, I. X. & Baker, R. (2021). *Stamped (for kids): Racism, antiracism, and you.* Little, Brown Books for Young Readers.

Christians, J. C. (2014). *Understanding the Black Flame and multigenerational education trauma: Toward a theory of dehumanization of Black students.* Lexington Books.

Cisneros, S. (1984). *The house on Mango Street.* Vintage.

Coates, T.-N. (2015). *Between the world and me.* Spiegel & Grau.

Cochran-Smith, M. & Lytle, S. (2009). *Inquiry as stance: Practitioner research for the next generation.* Teachers College Press.

Collins, S. (2008). *The hunger games.* Scholastic Press.

Comber, B. & Simpson, A. (2001). *Negotiating critical literacies in classrooms.* Lawrence Erlbaum Associate Publishers.

Cramer, L. (2015). Inequities of intervention among culturally and linguistically diverse students. *Penn GSE Perspectives on Urban Education, 12*(1), 1–8.

Crawford-Garrett, K. & Riley, K. (2016). Living and learning in the here-and-now: Critical inquiry in literacy teacher education. *Journal of Language and Literacy Education, 12*(2), 33–55.

Crenshaw, K. W. (1989). Demarginalizing the intersection of race and sex: A Black feminist critique of antidiscrimination doctrine, feminist theory, and antiracist politics. In K. T. Bartlett & R. Kennedy (Eds.), *Feminist legal theory: Readings in law and gender.* Routledge.

Crenshaw, K. W., Gotanda, N., Peller, G. & Thomas, K. (Eds.). (1995). *Critical Race Theory: The key writings that formed the movement.* The New York Press.

Daniels, J. R. & Varghese, M. (2020). Troubling practice: Exploring the relationship between whiteness and practice-based teacher education in considering a raciolinguicized teacher subjectivity. *Educational Researcher, 49*(1), 56–63.

Darder, A., Baltodano, M. P. & Torres, R. D. (2009). *Critical pedagogy reader.* Routledge.

Darling-Hammond, L. (2015). Want to close the achievement gap? Close the teaching gap. *American Educator, 38*(4), 14–18.

Delgado, R. (1984). The imperial scholar: Reflections on a review of civil rights literature. *University of Pennsylvania Law Review, 132*(3), 561–578.

Delgado, R. & Stefancic, J. (2017). *Critical Race Theory: An introduction* (3rd ed.). NYU Press.

Delpit, L. (2013). *"Multiplication is for white people": Raising expectations for other people's children.* The New Press.

Delpit, L. (Ed.). (2019). *Teaching when the world is on fire.* The New Press.

Delpit, L. & Dowdy, J. K. (2008). *The skin that we speak: Thoughts on language and culture in the classroom.* The New Press.

Dewey, J. (1933). *How we think: A restatement of the relation of reflective thinking to the educative process.* D.C. Health.

Diez, M. E. & Murrell, P. C. (2010). *Teaching as a moral practice: Defining, developing, and assessing professional dispositions in teacher education.* Harvard Education Press.

Dixon, R. (2021). *From excluded to essential: Tracing the racist exclusion of farmworkers, domestic workers, and tipped workers from the Fair Labor Standards Act.* National Employment Law Project. https://docs.house.gov/meetings/ED/ED10/20210503/112535/HHRG-117-ED10-Wstate-DixonR-20210503.pdf

Donnelly, P. (2019). A new guide for guided reading: More guided, more reading. *Practical Literacy, 24*(1), 9–12.

Douglas, B. & Ballard, C. (2008). *Foreign bodies: Oceania and the science of race, 1750–1940.* Australian National University Press.

Du Plooy, L. L. (2019). The manifestations of the practice of within-class homogeneous ability grouping. *South African Journal of Childhood Education, 9*(1), 1–11.

Duke, N. K., Ward, A. E. & Pearson, P. D. (2021). The science of reading comprehension instruction. *The Reading Teacher, 74*(6), 663–672.

Dutro, E. (2009). Children writing "Hard Times": Lived experiences of poverty and the class-privileged assumptions of a mandated curriculum. *Language Arts, 87*(2), 89–98.

Edwards, P. A., McMillon, G. T. & Turner, J. D. (2010). *Change is gonna come: Transforming literacy education for African American students.* Teachers College Press.

Ehle, J. (1988). *Trail of tears: The rise and fall of the Cherokee Nation.* Anchor Books Doubleday.

Emdin, C. (2016). *For white folks who teach in the Hood . . . and the rest of y'all too: Reality pedagogy and urban education.* Beacon Press.

Erickson, F. (1987). Transformation and school success: The politics and culture of educational achievement. *Anthropology & Education Quarterly, 18*(4), 335–356.

Everett, S. & Moten, T. (2022). Looking back and learning forward: Cultivating robust literacy instruction and joy among Black elementary boys. *Language Arts, 99*(5), 313–324.

Ferdman, B. M. & Gallegos, P. I. (2001). Latinos and racial identity development. In C. L. Wijeyesinghe & B. W. Jackson III (Eds.). *New perspectives on racial identity development: A theoretical and practical anthology* (pp. 32–66). New York University Press.

Flores, N. & Rosa, J. (2015). Undoing appropriateness: Raciolinguistic ideologies and language diversity in education. *Harvard Educational Review, 85*, 149–171.

Freire, P. (1970). *Pedagogy of the oppressed.* Seabury Press.

Freire, P. (1973). *Education for critical consciousness.* Continuum Publishing.

Fu, D., Hadjioannou, X. & Zhou, X. (2019). *Translanguaging for emergent bilinguals: Inclusive teaching in the linguistically diverse classroom.* Teachers College Press.

García, O. (2009). *Bilingual education in the 21st century: A global perspective.* Wiley-Blackwell.

García, O. & Kleifgen, J. A. (2018). *Educating emergent bilinguals: Policies, programs, and practices for English learners.* Teachers College Press.

Gay, G. (2010). Acting on beliefs in teacher education for cultural diversity. *Journal of Teacher Education, 61*(1–2), 143–152.

Geiter, M. K. & Speck, W. A. (2002). *Colonial America: From Jamestown to Yorktown.* Red Globe Press.

Gilliam, W. S., Maupin, A. N., Reyes, C. R., Accavitti, M. & Shic, F. (2016). *Do early educators' implicit biases regarding sex and race relate to behavior expectations and recommendations of preschool expulsions and suspensions? Research study brief.* Yale Child Study Center, Yale University.

Gilliam, W. S. & Shahar, G. (2006). Preschool and child care expulsion and suspension: Rates and predictors in one state. *Infants & Young Children, 19,* 228–245.

Giroux, H. (1987). Introduction: Literacy and the pedagogy of political empowerment. In P. Freire & D. Macedo (Eds.), *Literacy: Reading the word & the world* (pp. 1–27). Bergin & Garvey.

González, N., Moll, L. C. & Amanti, C. (Eds.). (2005). *Funds of knowledge: Theorizing practices in households, communities, and classrooms.* Lawrence Erlbaum Associates Publishers.

Government Accounting Office [GAO]. (2022, June 16). *K–12 education: Student population has significantly diversified, but many schools remain divided along racial, ethnic, and economic lines* (GAO Publication No. 22-104737). https://www.gao.gov/products/gao-22-104737

Graham, S., Liu, X., Aitken, A., Ng, C., Bartlett, B., Harris, K. R. & Holzapfel, J. (2018). Effectiveness of literacy programs balancing reading and writing instruction: A meta-analysis. *Reading Research Quarterly, 52*(2), 279–304.

Greene, D. T. (2020). "Black female literacy teachers are our school parents!!": Academic othermothering depicted in multicultural young adult texts. *Journal of Language and Literacy Education, 16*(1), 1–19.

Greene, D. T. (2021). From bottom bitch to top literary scholar: Academic othermothering depicted in a young adult street literature memoir text. *Research on Diversity in Youth Literature, 4*(1), 1–23.

Grissom, A. & Redding, C. (2016). Discretion and disproportionality: Explaining the underrepresentation of high-achieving students of color in gifted programs. *AERA Open, 2*(1).

Gross Cheliotes, L. & Reilly, M. F. (2010). *Coaching conversations: Transforming your school one conversation at a time.* SAGE Publications.

Gutiérrez, K. D. & Lee, C. (2009). Robust informal learning environments for youth from non-dominant groups and implications for literacy learning in formal schooling. In L. Morrow, R. Rueda & D. Lapp (Eds.), *Handbook of research on literacy instruction: Issues of diversity, policy, and equity.* Guilford.

Gutiérrez, K. D. & Rogoff, B. (2003). Cultural ways of learning. *Educational Researcher, 32,* 19–25.

Haddix, M. (2009). Black boys can write: Challenging dominant framings of African American adolescent males in literacy research. *Journal of Adolescent & Adult Literacy, 53*(4), 341–343.

Harrison, R. (2021). *Black hands, White House: Slave labor and the making of America.* Fortress Press.

Hart, B. & Risley, T. R. (1995). *Meaningful differences in the everyday experience of young American children*. Brookes.

Heath, S. B. (1982). What no bedtime story means: Narrative skills at home and school. *Language in Society, 11*(1), 49–76.

Heath, S. B. (1983). *Ways with words: Language, life, and work in communities and classrooms*. Cambridge University Press.

Heffernan, L. (2004). *Critical literacy and writer's workshop*. International Reading Association.

Helms, J. E. (1995). An update of Helm's white and people of color racial identity models. In J. G. Ponterotto, J. M. Casa, L. S. Suzuki & C. M. Alexander (Eds.), *Handbook of multicultural counseling* (pp. 181–198). SAGE Publications.

Hoffman, J. V. (2017). What if "just right" is just wrong? The unintended consequences of leveling readers. *The Reading Teacher, 71*(3), 265–273.

Hoffman, J. V., Cabell, S. Q., Barrueco, S., Hollins, E. R. & Pearson, P. D. (2020). Critical issues in the science of reading: Striving for a wide-angle view in research. *Literacy Research: Theory, Method, and Practice, 70*, 87–105.

Hsieh, B. & Kim, J. (2020). Challenging the invisibility of Asian Americans in education. *Review of Education, Pedagogy, and Cultural Studies, 42*(2), 95–103.

Hudelson, P. M. (2004). Culture and quality: An anthropological perspective. *International Journal for Quality in Health Care, 16*(5), 345–346.

Husband, T. & Kang, G. (2020). Identifying promising literacy practices for Black males in P–12 classrooms: An integrative review. *Journal of Language and Literacy, 16*(1), 1–34.

Irvine, J. J. (2003). *Educating teachers for diversity: Seeing with a cultural eye.* Teachers College Press.

Jablonski, N. G. (2021). Skin color and race. *American Journal of Physical Anthropology, 175*(2), 437–447.

Janks, H. (2018). Texts, identities, and ethics: Critical literacy in a post-truth world. *Journal of Adolescent & Adult Literacy, 62*(1), 95–99.

Johanson, K. (2020, August 17). *Drugs, retaliation contributing to surge in Philadelphia shootings*. Retrieved from https://www.audacy.com/kywnewsradio/articles/news/drugs-gangs-contributing-to-surge-in-philadelphia-shootings

Johnson, L. P. & Sullivan, H. (2020). Revealing the human and the writer: The promise of a humanizing writing pedagogy for Black students. *Research in the Teaching of English, 54*(4), 418–438.

Kaufman, J. S., Jaser, S. S., Vaughan, E. L., Reynolds, J. S., Di Donato, J., Bernard, S. N. & Hernandez-Brereton, M. (2010). Patterns in office referral data by grade, race/ethnicity, and gender. *Journal of Positive Behavior Interventions, 12*, 44–54.

Kelley, R. D. G. (2003). Race: The power of an illusion. Episode 2: "The story we tell." California Newsreel. https://www.pbs.org/race/000_About/002_04-background-02-05.htm

Kendi, I. X. (2019). *How to be an antiracist.* Random House Publishing Group.

Kim, J. (2001). Asian American racial identity theory. In C. L. Wijeyesinghe & B. W. Jackson III (Eds.), *New perspectives on racial identity development: A theoretical and practical anthology* (pp. 138–161). New York University Press.

Kinloch, V., Penn, C. & Burkhard, T. (2020). Black Lives Matter: Storying, identities, and counternarratives. *Journal of Literacy Research, 52*(4), 382–405.

Kleinfeld, J. (1975). Effective teachers of Eskimo and Indian students. *The School Review, 83*(2), 301–344.

Kozol, J. (2006). *The shame of the nation: The restoration of apartheid schooling in America.* Three Rivers Press.

Ladson-Billings, G. (1995). Toward a theory of culturally relevant pedagogy. *American Educational Research Journal, 32*(3), 465–491.

Ladson-Billings, G. (2006). From the achievement gap to the education debt: Understanding achievement in U.S. schools. *Educational Researcher, 35*(7), 3–12.

Ladson-Billings, G. (2009). *The dreamkeepers: Successful teachers of African American children.* Jossey-Bass.

Ladson-Billings, G. & Dixson, A. (2022). Put some respect on the theory: Confronting distortions of culturally relevant pedagogy. In C. Compton-Lilly, T. L. Ellison, K. Perry & P. Smagorinsky (Eds.), *Whitewashed critical perspectives: Restoring the edge to edgy ideas* (pp. 122–137). Routledge.

Lankshear, C. & McLaren, P. L. (1993). *Critical literacy: Politics, praxis, and the postmodern.* SUNY Press.

Lazar, A. (2004). *Learning to be literacy teachers in urban classrooms: Stories of growth and change.* International Reading Association.

Lazar, A. (2022). Apprenticing for equity literacy teaching: A needed change in teacher education. *Journal of Literacy Research, 54*(2), 158–181.

Leonard, A. M. & Woodland, R. H. (2022). Anti-racism is not an initiative: How professional learning communities may advance equity and social–emotional learning in schools. *Theory into Practice, 61*(2), 212–223.

Leung, C. T. (2021). *What I see: Anti-Asian racism from the eyes of a child.* LegaC Publishing.

Lewis, C. (1993). "Give people a chance": Acknowledging social differences in reading. *Language Arts, 70*(6), 454–461.

Lewis, R. D. (2018). *When cultures collide: Leading across cultures.* Nicholas Brealey.

Lewison, M., Flint, A. S. & Van Sluys, K. (2002). Taking on critical literacy: The journey of newcomers and novices. *Language Arts, 79*(5), 382–392.

Love, B. L. (2019). *We want to do more than survive: Abolitionist teaching and the pursuit of educational freedom.* Beacon Press.

Macedo, S. (2000). *Diversity and distrust: Civic education in a multicultural democracy.* Harvard University Press.

Mandela, N. (1990, June 23). *Speech to Madison Park High School, Boston, MA.* Retrieved from https://www.youtube.com/watch?v=b66c6OkMZGw.

Matsuda, M. J. (1991). Voices of America: Accents, antidiscrimination law, and a jurisprudence for the last reconstruction. *The Yale Law Journal, 100*(5), 1329–1407.

Mau, R. Y. (1992). The validity and devolution of a concept: Student alienation. *Adolescence, 27*(107), 731–741.

McDaniel, C. (2006). *Critical literacy: A way of thinking, a way of life.* Peter Lang.

McIntosh, K., Moss, E., Nunn, R. & Shambaugh, J. (2020, February 27). *Examining the Black-white wealth gap.* Brookings. https://www.brookings.edu/blog/up-front/2020/02/27/examining-the-black-white-wealth-gap/

McLaren, P. (1994). *Life in schools: An introduction to critical pedagogy in the foundations of education* (2nd ed.). Longman.

McLean, C. A., Boling, E. C. & Rowsell, J. (2009). Engaging diverse students in multiple literacies in and out of school. In L. Morrow, R. Rueda & D. Lapp (Eds.), *Handbook of research on literacy instruction: Issues of diversity, policy, and equity*. Guilford.

Meacham, J. (2022). *And there was light: Abraham Lincoln and the American struggle*. Random House.

Milner, H. R., IV. (2015). *Rac(e)ing to class: Confronting poverty and race in schools and classrooms*. Harvard Education Press.

Milner, H. R., IV. (2017). Race, talk, opportunity gaps, and curriculum shifts in teacher education. *Literacy Research: Theory, Method, and Practice, 66*, 73–94.

Milner, H. R., IV. (2019). Race to improve teacher education: Building awareness for instruction practice. *American Educator, 43*(3), 13–17.

Milner, H. R., IV. (2020). Disrupting racism and whiteness in researching a science of reading. *Reading Research Quarterly, 55*(S1), S249–S253.

Mobe, T. (n.d.). *Eight African proverbs that every global citizen should know*. Global Citizen. https://www.globalcitizen.org/en/content/africa-proverbs-global-citizens-action-end-poverty/

Moll, L., Amanti, C. N. D. & González, N. (1992). Funds of knowledge for teaching: Using a qualitative to connect homes and schools. *Theory into Practice, 31*(2), 132–141.

Morrow, L. Rueda, R. & Lapp, D. (2009). *Handbook of research on literacy instruction: Issues of diversity, policy, and equity*. Guilford.

Muhammad, G. E. (2020). *Cultivating genius: An equity framework for culturally and historically responsive literacy*. Scholastic, Inc.

Muhammad, G. E. & Haddix, M. (2016). Centering Black girls' literacies: A review of literature on the multiple ways of knowing of Black girls. *English Education, 48*(4), 299–336.

National Council of Teachers of English [NCTE]. (2018). The Black girls' literacies collective statement. *Research in the Teaching of English, 53*(2), 173–175.

National Council of Teachers of English [NCTE]. (2020). *Literacy is more than just reading and writing*. Retrieved from https://ncte.org/blog/2020/03/literacy-just-reading-writing/

Nieto, S. (2000). *Affirming diversity: The sociopolitical context of multicultural education* (3rd ed.). Addison Wesley Longman, Inc.

Nieto, S. (2005). *Affirming diversity*. Pearson Education.

Oakes, J. & Lipton, M. (2002). *Teaching to change the world*. McGraw-Hill.

O'Dell, S. (1992). *Thunder rolling in the mountains*. Dell Yearling Paperback.

Paris, D. (2012). Culturally sustaining pedagogy: A needed change in stance, terminology, and practice. *Educational Researcher, 41*(3), 93–97.

Paris, D. & Alim, H. S. (2014). What are we seeking to sustain through culturally sustaining pedagogy? A loving critique forward. *Harvard Educational Review, 84*(1), 85–100.

Parks, R. & Reed, G. J. (1996). *Dear Mrs. Parks: A dialogue with today's youth*. Lee & Low Books.

Parsons, E. F. (2019). *Ku-Klux: The birth of the Klan during Reconstruction*. The University of North Carolina Press.

Patterson Williams, A. D., Higgs, J. M, Athanases, S. Z., Caraballo, L. & Martinez, D. C. (2020). Noticing for equity to sustain multilingual literacies. *Journal of Adolescent & Adult Literacy, 63*(4), 457–461.

Patton, L. D., Farmer-Hinton, R. L., Lewis, J. D. & Rivers, I. (2010). *"Dear Mr. Kozol": Four African American women scholars and the reauthoring of Savage Inequalities*. Paper presented at the annual meeting of the American Educational Research Association, Denver, CO.

Picower, B. (2021). *Reading, writing, and racism: Disrupting whiteness in teacher education and the classroom*. Beacon Press.

Pierson, R. (2013, May). *Every kid needs a champion*. [Video]. TED Conferences. https://www.ted.com/talks/rita_pierson_every_kid_needs_a_champion?language=en

Plough, B. & Garcia, R. (2015). Whole school English learner reform: A heuristic approach to professional learning in middle schools. *Planning and Changing, 46*(1), 21–41.

Poston, W. S. C. (1990). The biracial identity development model: A needed addition. *Journal of Counseling and Development, 69*(2), 152–155.

Price-Dennis, D. & Muhammad, G. E. (2021). *Black girl's literacies: Transforming lives and literacy practices*. Routledge.

Price-Dennis, D. & Sealy-Ruiz, Y. (2021). *Advancing racial literacies in teacher education: Activism for equity in digital spaces*. Teachers College Press.

Purcell-Gates, V. (1996). Stories, coupons, and the *TV Guide*: Relationships between home literacy experiences and emergent literacy knowledge. *Reading Research Quarterly, 31*(4), 406–428.

Reece, R. L. (2019). Color crit: Critical *Race Theory* and the history and future of colorism in the United States. *Journal of Black Studies, 50*(1), 3–25.

Roberts, M. A. (2010). Toward a theory of culturally relevant critical teacher care: African American teachers' definitions and perceptions of care for African American students. *Journal of Moral Education, 39*(4), 449–467.

Rodriguez, J. P. (2006). Encyclopedia of Slave Resistance and Rebellion [2 volumes]: Greenwood Milestones in African American History. Greenwood.

Rogers, R. & Mosley, M. (2006). Racial literacy in a second-grade classroom: Critical Race Theory, whiteness studies and literacy research. *Reading Research Quarterly, 41*(4), 462–495.

Rolon-Dow, R. (2005). Critical care: A color(full) analysis of care narratives in the schooling experiences of Puerto Rican girls. *American Educational Research Journal, 42*(1), 77–111.

Rosa, J. & Flores, N. (2017). Unsettling race and language: Toward a raciolinguistic perspective. *Language in Society, 46*(5), 621–647.

Rosales, J. & Walker, T. (2021). The racist beginnings of standardized testing. National Education Association. Retrieved from https://www.nea.org/advocating-for-change/new-from-nea/racist-beginnings-standardized-testing

Sachs, J. (2022). *Steep rise in gag orders, many sloppily drafted*. Pen America. https://pen.org/steep-rise-gag-orders-many-sloppily-drafted/

Saint-Louis, T. (2023, January 4). *Best female rappers of 2022*. HipHopDX. https://hiphopdx.com/editorials/best-female-rappers-of-2022

Schussler, D. L. (2006). Defining dispositions: Wading through murky waters. *The Teacher Educator, 41*(4), 251–268.

Sealy-Ruiz, Y. (2021). The critical literacy of race: Toward racial literacy in urban teacher education. In *Handbook of urban education* (pp. 281–295). Routledge.

Seaton, E. K. (2009). Perceived racial discrimination and racial identity profiles among African American adolescents. *Cultural Diversity and Ethnic Minority Psychology, 15*(2), 137.

Shollenberger, T. L. (2015). Racial disparities in school suspension and subsequent outcomes: Evidence from the National Longitudinal Study of Youth. In D. J. Losen (Ed.), *Closing the school discipline gap: Equitable remedies for excessive exclusion* (pp. 31–43). New York: Teachers College Press.

Siddle Walker, V. (1996). *The highest potential: An African American school community in the segregated South.* Chapel Hill, NC: The University of North Carolina Press.

Siddle Walker, V. (2001). African American teacher in the South: 1940–1960. *American Educational Research Journal, 38*(4), 751–779.

Skiba, R. J., Michael, R. S., Nardo, A. C. & Peterson, R. L. (2002). The color of discipline: Sources of racial and gender disproportionality in school punishment. *The Urban Review, 34*, 317–342.

Smith, C. (2021). *How the word is passed: A reckoning with the history of slavery across America.* Little, Brown, & Company.

Smith, P. (2020). "How does a Black person speak English?": Beyond American language norms. *American Educational Research Journal, 57*(1), 106–147.

Souto-Manning, M. (2021). Bridging the teacher education debt: A matter of justice. *Journal of Literacy Research, 53*(4), 588–600.

Sperry, D. E., Sperry, L. L. & Miller, P. J. (2019). Reexamining the verbal environments of children from different socioeconomic backgrounds. *Child Development, 90*(4), 1303–1318.

Stevens, L. P. & Bean, T. W. (2007). *Critical literacy: Context, research, and practice in the K–12 classroom.* SAGE Publications, Inc.

Street, B. (1984). *Literacy in theory and practice.* Cambridge University Press.

Stubbs, T. (2018). *Masters of violence: The plantation overseers of eighteenth-century Virginia, South Carolina, and Georgia (the Carolina Lowcountry and the Atlantic world).* University of South Carolina Press.

Tatum, A. W. (2009). *Reading for the life: (Re)building textual lineages of African American males.* Heinemann.

Tatum, A. W. (2014). Orienting African American male adolescents toward meaningful exchanges with texts. *Journal of Education, 94*(1), 35–47.

Thompkins-Bigelow, J. (2020). *Your name is a song.* The Innovation Press.

U.N. Climate Change. (December 10, 2018). *Greta Thunberg at COP24: "You are never too small to make a difference."* [Video]. https://www.youtube.com/watch?v=CAJuX7xed8o

U.S. Department of Education (n.d.). *Academic performance outcomes for English Learners.* Retrieved from https://www2.ed.gov/datastory/el-outcomes/index.html#one

Valenzuela, A. (1999). *Subtractive schooling: U.S.–Mexican youth and the politics of caring.* State University of New York Press.

Valenzuela, A. (Ed.). (2016). *Growing critically conscious teachers: A social justice curriculum for educators of Latino/a youth.* Teachers College Press.

Vandiver, B. J., Fhagen-Smith, P. E., Cokley, K. O., Cross Jr., W. E. & Worrell, F. C. (2001). Cross's nigrescence model: From theory to scale to theory. *Journal of Multicultural Counseling and Development, 29*(3), 174–200.

Vasquez, V. (2003). *Getting beyond "I like the book": Creating space for critical literacy in K–6 classrooms.* International Reading Association.

Vasquez, V. (2004). *Negotiating critical literacies with young children.* Lawrence Erlbaum.

Vile, J. (2022, November 22). *Stop W.O.K.E. Act (Florida) (2022).* The First Amendment Encyclopedia. https://mtsu.edu/first-amendment/article/2167/stop-w-o-k-e-act-florida

Vygotsky, L. (1978). *Mind in society: The development of high psychological processes.* Harvard University Press.

Wegrzyn, K. M. (2022). Opening up spaces to ask "Why?": Children discussing race and racism. (29992366) [Doctoral Dissertation, The University of Georgia]. ProQuest Dissertations & Thesis Global. https://ezproxy.sju.edu/login?url=https://www.proquest.com/dissertations-theses/opening-up-spaces-ask-why-children-discussing/docview/2773025053/se-2?accountid=14071

Wells, M. S., Morrison, J. D. & López-Robertson, J. (2022). Building critical reading and critical literacy with picturebook analysis. *The Reading Teacher, 76*(2), 191–200.

Wenger-Trayner, E. & Wenger-Trayner, B. (2015). *Introduction to communities of practice: A brief overview of the concept and its uses.* Retrieved from https://www.wenger-trayner.com/wp-content/uploads/2022/06/15-06-Brief-introduction-to-communities-of-practice.pdf

Wetzel, M. (2020). Disrupting race-evasive practices in literacy teacher education: Reflections on research and implications for policy. *Language Arts, 97*(5), 306–316.

Wharton-McDonald, R., Rankin, J. & Mistretta, J. (1997). Effective primary-grades literacy instruction equals balanced literacy instruction. *The Reading Teacher, 50*(6), 518.

Whipp, J. L. (2014). Developing caring with political clarity in high-poverty schools. In *American Educational Research Association Conference, 2014.* American Educational Research Association.

Whipp, J. L. (2016). Factors supporting teachers who practice critical care in urban schools. In *American Educational Research Association Poster Session, 2016.* American Educational Research Association.

Wilkerson, I. (2011). *The warmth of other suns: The epic story of America's great migration.* Vintage.

Williams, P. (1987). Spirit-murdering the messenger: The discourse of fingerpointing as the law's response to racism. *University of Miami Law Review, 42*(1), 127–157.

Williams-Garcia, R. (2011). *One crazy summer.* Thorndike Press Large Print.

Willis, A. I. (2019). Race, response to intervention, and reading research. *Journal of Literacy Research, 51*(4), 394–419.

Winfield, L. F. (1986). Teacher beliefs toward academically at risk students in inner urban schools. *The Urban Review, 18*(4), 253–268.

Wolff, R. D. (2016). How capitalism and racism support each other. Truthout. https://bannekerinstitute.fas.harvard.edu/files/bannekerinstitute/files/how_capitalism_and_racism_support_each_other.pdf

Wood, A. L. (2011). *Lynching and spectacle: Witnessing racial violence in America, 1890–1940*. The University of North Carolina Press.

Wright, B. L. & Counsell, S. L. (2018). *The brilliance of Black boys: Cultivating school success in the early grades*. Teachers College Press.

Wright, Z. (2022). *Dismantling a broken system: Actions to bridge the opportunity, equity, and justice gap in American education*. Solution Tree Press.

Yosso, T. J. (2005). Whose culture has capital?: A Critical Race Theory discussion of community cultural wealth. *Race, Ethnicity, and Education, 8*(1), 69–91.

Zeichner, K. M. (2009). *Teacher education and the struggle for social justice*. Routledge.

Index

About the Authors

Althier M. Lazar is a professor in the Teacher Education Department at Saint Joseph's University in Philadelphia. Her research focuses on understanding the ways teacher candidates acquire the dispositions and skills needed to see and nurture children's literate development. She has authored, coauthored, and edited several books, including *Culturally Sustaining Literacy Pedagogies: Honoring Students' Heritages, Literacies, and Languages* (2022), *Schools of Promise for Multilingual Students* (2018), *New Teachers in Urban Schools: Journeys Toward Social Equity Teaching* (2016), and *Bridging Literacy and Equity: The Essential Guide to Social Equity Teaching* (2012). She has also published numerous articles and book chapters on the topics of teacher growth and literacy teaching for social equity. Dr. Lazar received her PhD from the University of Pennsylvania.

Kaitlin K. Moran is an assistant professor in the Teacher Education Department at Saint Joseph's University in Philadelphia. Her research focuses broadly on improving outcomes for children and families through community-engaged, social-justice–centered scholarship. The lines of inquiry that she explores include pre-service teachers' and practicing teachers' advocacy orientations, early intervention and early childhood special education systems, and high-quality early childhood education and school programming. She has published articles on these lines of inquiry in journals such as *Urban Education, Topics in Early Childhood Special Education*, and the *Journal of Early Intervention. Connecting Equity, Literacy, and Language: Pathways Toward Advocacy-Focused Teaching* is her first book. Dr. Moran received her PhD from Temple University.

Shoshanna Edwards-Alexander is a clinical assistant professor of social work in the Department of Educational Leadership and Counseling at Saint Joseph's University in Philadelphia. Her research focuses on understanding the relationship between intersectionality and equity within organizations. She is also a diversity, equit,y and inclusion (DEI) strategist who leads seminars, designs and facilitates training programs, and evaluates how inclusive workplace spaces are. Dr. Edwards-Alexander is a licensed clinician, and she received her EdD from Saint Joseph's University.

